BECOMING A
REFLECTIVE
TEACHER

BECOMING A REFLECTIVE TEACHER

Leonard Kochendorfer

INTERACTIVE
RESOURCES
S E R I E S

AN NEA PROFESSIONAL LIBRARY PUBLICATION
NATIONAL EDUCATION ASSOCIATION
Washington, D.C.

Copyright © 1994 by National Education Association of the United States
Printing History
First Printing: July 1994

Note: The opinions expressed in this publication should not be construed as representing the policy or position of the National Education Association. Materials published by the NEA Professional Library are intended to be discussion documents for educators who are concerned with specialized interests of the profession.

This book is printed on acid-free paper.

Library of Congress Cataloging-in-Publication Data

Kochendorfer, Leonard
    Becoming a reflective teacher / Leonard Kochendorfer
    p. cm. — (Interactive resources)
    "An NEA professional library publication."
    Includes bibliographical references.
    ISBN 0-8106-3352-3
    1. Teaching—Handbooks, manuals, etc. 2. Action research in education—United States—
Handbooks, manuals, etc. 3. Teachers—United States—Handbooks, manuals, etc. I. Title II. Series.
LB1025.3.K64 1994
371.1'02—dc20   93-23714
                                                                                         CIP
                                                                                         Rev.

Contents

CHAPTER 1   OPENING SPACES. 11

Reading and Using This Book 11

Working with Others 12

Setting Up Meeting Procedures 13

The Content of the Meetings 13

CHAPTER 2   EXPLORING AUTOBIOGRAPHY 15

Strategy 2-1: Past Meanings of Teaching 15

Strategy 2-2: Significant Stories from Your Education 19

Strategy 2-3: Significant Teaching Stories 24

Strategy 2-4: Significant Teachers 27

Strategy 2-5: RepGridding Your Teachers 27

Strategy 2-6: Patterns in Your RepGrid 31

Strategy 2-7: Quantifying Your RepGrid 31

Strategy 2-8: Extending Teacher RepGrids 32

Strategy 2-9: Significant Others 34

Strategy 2-10: Writing Your Autobiography 35

Strategy 2-11: I Used to Be a Teacher Who 38

References 40

CHAPTER 3   EXAMINING CURRENT TEACHING. 41

Strategy 3-1: Journals to Record What I Do 41

Strategy 3-2: Continuum of Competence 43

Strategy 3-3: Going Beyond Teaching with the Competence Continuum **48**

Strategy 3-4: Graphs and Maps **49**

Strategy 3-5: Describing Other Feelings **49**

Strategy 3-6: It Is with Mixed Feelings **51**

Strategy 3-7: RepGridding Some Students **51**

Strategy 3-8: Patterns in Your RepGrid **54**

Strategy 3-9: Types of Intelligence **55**

Strategy 3-10: Changing Students **56**

Strategy 3-11: Theoretical Bases for Teaching Approaches **60**

Strategy 3-12: I Am the Kind of Teacher Who **61**

Strategy 3-13: Teaching As an "F" Word **67**

Strategy 3-14: I Used to Be a Teacher Who **73**

Strategy 3-15: Why I Am Doing This **73**

References **74**

CHAPTER 4   READING YOUR METAPHORS

CHAPTER 4   **READING YOUR METAPHORS** **75**

Metaphors in Education **76**

Strategy 4-1: Searching for Your Metaphors of Teaching **79**

Strategy 4-2: A Search for an Occupational Metaphor **80**

Strategy 4-3: A Metaphor Influenced by a Significant Teacher **80**

Strategy 4-4: A Significant Other's Metaphor **81**

Strategy 4-5: Metaphors from Your Autobiography **82**

Strategy 4-6: Journal Metaphors...**82**

Strategy 4-7: Switch Your Training...**83**

Strategy 4-8: RepGridding Occupations...**84**

Strategy 4-9: RepGridding Additional Occupations **87**

Strategy 4-10: Learning from Your Rituals **89**

Strategy 4-11: Take It Literally...**90**

Strategy 4-12: Reverse the Metaphor..**92**

Strategy 4-13: Mixed Metaphors..**93**

Strategy 4-14: Matched Metaphors **95**

Strategy 4-15: I Used to Be a Teacher Who...**96**

Strategy 4-16: Why I Am Doing This..**97**

References **98**

CHAPTER 5   HEARING YOUR STUDENTS

CHAPTER **5**   **HEARING YOUR STUDENTS**..**99**

Strategy 5-1: Student Constructs **100**

Strategy 5-2: School Groups...**101**

Strategy 5-3: Getting Some Culture **102**

Strategy 5-4: Important Knowledge **103**

Strategy 5-5: Important Aspects of Subjects...**104**

References **104**

CHAPTER 6   THREE APPROACHES TO RESEARCH 105

      An Example of Traditional Educational Research 105

      Traditional Educational Research Described 107

      An Example of Classroom Teacher Research 109

      Classroom Teacher Research Described 110

      An Example of Teacher-Based Action Research 111

      Teacher-Based Action Research Described 113

      Is T-BAR for You? 115

      A Few Words of Caution 116

CHAPTER 7   STARTING WITH T-BAR 117

      Why a Group? 117

      Using the Strategies 119

      Choosing a Theme 119

      Designing Action Plans 121

      Checking Your Plan for Ethics and T-BAR Traits 122

      Collecting Data 123

      Implementing Your Action Plan 126

      Strategy 7-1: An Ethical Comparison by the T-BAR Group 126

      Strategy 7-2: An Ethical Self-Check 127

      Strategy 7-3: Rate Your Project 128

Strategy 7-4: Choosing Data Collection Techniques **128**

Strategy 7-5: Group Validity Check **128**

Strategy 7-6: Group Data Collection Critique. **130**

CHAPTER 8 REFLECTING ON YOUR RESEARCH 131

Reflection en Route **131**

Travelers' Innocence **131**

How Valid an Experience? **132**

A New Itinerary **133**

Regrouping for Action **133**

When the Road Ends **133**

Compiling a Travelogue. **133**

That Others May Follow. **135**

Metaphor's End **136**

Strategy 8-1: Group In-Progress Meeting 1 ....**136**

Strategy 8-2: Group In-Progress Meeting 2. ....**137**

Strategy 8-3: Compiling Insights. **139**

Strategy 8-4: A New Direction **141**

Strategy 8-5: Checking the Logic of Your Report. **141**

ANNOTATED READINGS 143

The Author   Leonard Kochendorfer has taught at the elementary, middle, and high school levels. At the university level, he has worked with both student teachers and veteran classroom teachers. In recent years he has devoted full time to teaching and research in the middle school—teaching math and science classes, researching the practice of other middle school teachers, and serving on a school advisory council. His next project is an exploration of the reflective processes of experienced middle school teachers. He is using extensive classroom observations and interviews with four teachers to describe for novice teachers the skills and knowledge that experienced teachers call upon when they reflect on their teaching.

Advisory Panel

Linda A. Bacon
Library Media Specialist
Pinellas Technical Education Center
Clearwater, Florida

Katherine A. Brill
Language Arts Teacher
Krueger Junior High School
Michigan City, Indiana

Debbie Catley
Special Education Chairperson
Myrtle Beach Elementary
Myrtle Beach, South Carolina

Iginio Fontana
Elementary School Teacher
Shearer School
Napa, California

Robert E. Johnson
Professor of Education
University of North Alabama
Florence, Alabama

Carrol K. Harrison
Learning Disability Specialist
Hartley School
Portland, Oregon

David M. Silverstone
Retired Professor of Educational
Management and Public
Administration and Director of
Audiovisual Center
University of Bridgeport
Bridgeport, Connecticut

Kevin J. Swick
Professor of Education and
Coordinator of the Specialist in
Teaching Degree Program
University of South Carolina
Columbia, South Carolina

CHAPTER 1

....

OPENING SPACES

Is this book written for you? It is if you see yourself in the following constellation of traits:

• Others see you as hardworking, successful, and inspired, but privately you know that you are not getting the kind of results you want.

• You realize that when more of the same no longer works, it is time to change.

• You leave inservice workshops with the uncomfortable feeling that the skills presented were not really what you wanted.

• You do not believe that you can resolve the problems you face just by choosing and using the right combination of the right techniques.

• You are uncomfortable with the allegation that the failure of America's economy is due to the failure of your students, which is due to your failure as a teacher.

• You do not accept the idea that the solutions to your students' problems can be found only in the work of researchers who employ objective methods on large groups of students.

• You believe that the people who teach should be at least some of the people who examine teaching.

This book can help you reflect on and challenge what is given to you. Reflection helps you to be critical.

The word *critical* may sound rather negative at first. It is true that some criticism can be quite negative. It usually is negative, for example, when the critic speaks without careful prior reflection, when the critic's words are not based on sufficient experience, or when the critic opposes ideas solely because of the source of those ideas.

This book uses the term *criticism* in a very different sense. Criticism of ideas and practices—your own and others'—is a positive process when you base the critical judgment on an awareness of your actions and the deep sense of correctness that comes from reflection.

The strategies presented here can help you to identify what you believe and examine what you are doing. The process will help bring to a conscious level what you know in a deep, intuitive sense to be true. As a result, you will become more confident in the rightness of what you know, you will be better able to discern and defend best practice, and you will have a clearer sense of what is valuable for you and how you might achieve it.

Working through the strategies will also make you aware of areas that you would like to change. The reflective process opens spaces in your imagination, spaces where you can entertain new possibilities, ask questions, and speak about what you believe to be right.

In the course of this reflection and challenge, you can take your destiny out of the hands of others and put it into your own hands. You can become your own trusted change agent.

Be forewarned, though. Reflection can get you into trouble with yourself. By keeping your teaching open to review, you will keep yourself somewhat uncomfortable. You may become pleased with what you do and the effects it produces, but you will never be completely satisfied. You will, however, be confident that you are doing your best—and that your best will get better.

Reading and Using This Book

The strategies described in the first five chapters of *Becoming A Reflective Teacher* are designed to help you reflect on and challenge your concepts of schools and teaching. You can then investigate the validity of your conclusions by using the model of teacher-based action research (T-BAR), which is described in the last three chapters.

There is an inherent logic in the order of the chapters in this book, but following that logic is much less important than meeting your needs. You might begin by reading over Chapters 2 and 3 and using some strategies described in those chapters. Then you could scan Chapters 4 and 5 for other strategies that seem applicable to your particular needs. Working for several months with the strategies in these early chapters will be valuable preparation for applying the ideas on research described in Chapters 6, 7, and 8.

Suggested activities are easy to identify because the first three words of the directions are in boldface italics.

An annotated list of readings follows Chapter 8. Reading some of these materials may be quite helpful. The option is there for you.

By all means, though, as you work through the strategies, *keep everything you write*. Doing so will help you in the future, since certain strategies call for you to look back and reflect again on what you have developed.

Working With Others

While working through these strategies in isolation might be beneficial, you are likely to learn much more about yourself as a teacher and about your working situations if you join in this process with a small group of colleagues. Being critical of yourself is difficult, and questioning old habits can be painful. Continuous support from caring others is almost a necessity for you to keep the process moving.

The group has two primary purposes. One is to serve as a prop. By supporting one another, everyone can gain strength at those times when it is difficult to move forward alone. A second purpose of the group is to act as a mirror. When your thoughts are reflected back to you, you are likely to gain new perspectives.

Not just any group is ideal, however. Some groups may hinder more than help. If some members of your group interfere with its sup-port and reflection functions and deny the space you need for honest questioning, the group is not likely to help you become a critical teacher.

Your best chance for success lies in developing a group that has these five characteristics:

• *Small size.* Five members is optimal, but groups with two to eight members are workable.

• *Equality of position.* Someone with the power of position is inclined to dominate others in the group. For this reason, it is not generally a good idea to have the professor of your course, an administrator in your school, or your supervisor as a member of the group.

• *Equality of expertise.* Are you about as likely to help each of the others in your group as each of them is likely to help you? Although it is not necessary for everyone in the group to have similar training and experience, it is important that no one be seen as the constant helper or the constant recipient of help.

• *Equality of openness.* Are you as likely to disclose information to others as they are to be open with you? Of course it is important for each group member to be an attentive listener, but each should also be prepared to contribute personal reflections to the group.

• *Equality of commitment.* All parties should join the group because they want to become critical of their own teaching. No one should join because of a sense of obligation or the desire to be viewed favorably by others.

This description of a perfectly egalitarian group is an ideal not likely to be matched in the real world. It is simply a goal toward which to strive. Significant deviations from this model, however, are likely to cause problems for the group. At some point, those problems will have to be solved. That experience can be positive, but remember, the main objective for meeting in a group is to help each of you become a reflective teacher. Having members in your group who are consistently unable to make a positive contribution will not help and may impede other group members who are trying to reach that objective.

Setting Up Meeting Procedures

At the initial meetings, the group must discuss and establish the kind and degree of structure needed. By reaching a consensus on procedural issues, and by discussing them again if your initial agreements fail to work the way you want, you can ease the work of your group.

Some important points to consider include:

• How strongly do you want to enforce a starting time? In general, purposeful meetings usually start at the agreed upon time.

• What does *on time* mean? If members find it difficult to arrive on time, perhaps the group needs to set a more realistic starting time.

• Will you wait for latecomers?

• Will you search out members who do not arrive on time? If someone does search halls, classrooms, and lounges for group members, you might find that members come to depend upon such personal attention.

• What does the group do when someone comes after the meeting begins? One possible scenario is that they arrive quietly, and as soon as there is a natural break, they are greeted and filled in on what has gone on already.

• What are legitimate reasons for missing a meeting?

• Should group members notify someone if they must miss a meeting? If so, who should be informed?

• Should members attend if they are not prepared?

• If a member needs to leave a meeting early, when should that fact be made known? Naturally, if plans for an early departure are mentioned at the beginning of the meeting, the group can decide whether to adjourn when one member leaves or continue to the regular ending time.

• Under what circumstances can one be called away from the meeting? If leaving is permissible only in emergencies, the group will have to define *emergency*.

While the group should not have a standing chairperson, someone should act as convener for each meeting. The convener's responsibilities logically include:

• calling the meeting to order,
• presenting a proposed agenda,
• keeping the group on task, and
• seeing that the meeting ends on time.

The Content of the Meetings

In each meeting, try to accomplish whatever you have decided to do in the time you have available. Be flexible, making changes when there is a need to do so.

You might begin each session with each group member briefly recounting something worth celebrating that happened since the last meeting. A cognitively oriented person might describe an incident that provided food for thought or led to understanding, insight, or a meeting of the minds. Someone to whom relationship is important could describe a connection made, a mutual awareness, or a way of reaching another person. Sometimes metaphors convey ideas especially well, too. For example, if a football metaphor has meaning for you, you could describe a victory, touchdown, extra point, or clean tackle.

Generally, as the group members talk about their experiences, each one sets an agenda for that segment of the meeting. What this idea means in practice is that each speaker delineates the kind and degree of feedback, if any, that is wanted from other group members. To establish such parameters, an individual's contribution can begin with openers like these:

• I'd like you to listen to my thoughts, please, without making any comments or asking any questions.

• I'd like to know if what I am going to say makes any sense to you.

• See if you can relate to this incident.

• I'm wondering if you would have done what I did.

• Is there another way I might have handled this situation?

• Does this event help you see some message about my teaching that I apparently don't see?

When a person wants no more feedback, a simple "Thanks, guys" or "That's enough" should immediately end everyone's comments. Requests like these should always be heeded and respected. If one member continues to give feedback after such a request, another member should quickly remind the violator that feedback must cease.

To conclude meetings, the group might:

• *Summarize.* Group members might, in a few sentences, sum up what each of them sees as personal or group insights.

• *Choose strategies for your next meeting.* Move around chapters freely. Have several strategies going on at once, if it seems appropriate to do so.

• *Choose your next meeting place and time.*

• *Choose a convener for the next meeting.* Between meetings, the next designated convener could be responsible for working out necessary changes in meeting times and topics, for answering group members' questions, and for receiving notification from members who are going to miss the next meeting.

The process of becoming a reflective teacher is not likely to be easy. The time and personal energy you invest can be costly. The obstacles you face in just getting your group organized may make you wonder whether the ultimate effects will be worth the effort.

But take heart. The work of getting started and the confusion of your first several meetings are likely to pay off soon in increased collegiality and the new spaces that will open to you. These gains will encourage you to continue.

At this point, I suggest that you scan the rest of the chapters to get a more thorough picture of what is ahead, and give copies of this book to some of your trusted colleagues. Ask them to look it over and to consider joining you in an eventful journey—becoming a reflective teacher.

CHAPTER 2

EXPLORING AUTOBIOGRAPHY

The eleven strategies in this chapter are designed to help you recall and reflect upon the specific past events that led you to teaching. This focused remembering process is beneficial because why you became a teacher influences who you are now as a teacher.

You probably could say why you teach in a simple sentence, but simple answers are not likely to be complete answers. The varied and complex motives of good teachers have grown from unique collections of life experiences. Bringing these experiences to your awareness and reflecting on them will make you more conscious of exactly why you teach. It will also help you understand why no one else in your school is quite like you.

Strategy 2-1
PAST MEANINGS

The purpose of this strategy is to help you become aware of how your definition of teaching has changed over time.

For You

Write conclusions to each of the following incomplete statements. The more detail you include, the more insights you are likely to gain later.

1. When I first decided to become a teacher, I thought that *to teach* meant...

_____

_____

_____

2. Just before my student teaching, *to teach* meant...

_____

_____

_____

3. Just after student teaching, *to teach* meant...

_____

_____

_____

4. At the end of my first semester of teaching, *to teach* meant...

_____

_____

_____

5. At the beginning of my second year, *to teach* meant...

_____

_____

_____

6. Now, *to teach* means...

_____

_____

_____

Use the preceding answers to fill in the boxes in Figure 2.1. In the first box of the "Changes" column, write the changes in your definition of what it means to teach that occurred between the time you first decided to teach and when you began student teaching (use your answers 1 and 2). Below that, record the changes between the beginning and end of student teaching (answer 3), the changes between the end of student teaching and the end of your first semester of teaching (answer 4), the changes between the end of the first semester of teaching and the beginning of the second year (answer 5), and the changes between the second year of teaching and now (answer 6).

In the "Cause" column, record what you think may have caused each of these changes. In the "Gained" column, show what you gained with each change. In the "Lost" column, indicate what was lost. In the "Want to Recover" column, specify what you would like to recover from what was lost.

For the Group   *Summarize in writing* how your definition of teaching has changed with time and experience. Share your summary with the group. Ask members of the group to tell you how the changes in your definitions are similar to theirs.

_____

_____

_____

_____

_____

_____

	Changes	Cause	Gained	Lost	Want to recover
Up to. . . Student teaching					
End of student teaching					
End of first semester of teaching					
Start of second year of teaching					
Now					

Strategy 2-2

SIGNIFICANT
STORIES FROM
YOUR EDUCATION

This strategy is designed to help you recall an early event (one that occurred before you finished high school) that was significant in your decision to teach.

For You *Write your first* response to each item below. Jot down just enough words to identify the event so that you can recall it later.

- The specific event that pops into my head when I think of:

1. school—

_____

_____

_____

2. teacher—

_____

_____

_____

3. classroom—

_____

_____

_____

4. books—

_____

_____

_____

5. learning—

_____

_____

_____

• The time I felt:

1. competent—

_____

_____

_____

_____

2. embarrassed—

_____

_____

_____

3. stupid—

_____

_____

_____

4. warm—

_____

_____

_____

_____

5. small—

_____

_____

_____

_____

6. praised—

_____

_____

_____

_____

7. hurt—

_____

_____

_____

_____

Put a check by those events that relate in some way to your decision to teach (even though the actual decision to teach may have come much later). Choose one of the checked events and write a story about it in some detail.

_____

_____

_____

_____

_____

_____

_____

_____

_____

_____

_____

_____

_____

_____

_____

_____

_____

_____

_____

_____

_____

_____

_____

_____

_____

_____

_____

_____

_____

_____

_____

_____

_____

_____

_____

For the Group *Read your story* to your group, but do not tell them how it is related to your decision to teach. Ask if others have had a similar experience. If so, ask each to describe that experience to the group and to relate what meaning it had. Then let the group know what meaning your experience had for you and how it is related to your decision to teach.

Strategy 2-3
SIGNIFICANT
TEACHING STORIES

This strategy is designed to reveal insights about teaching that have occurred to you since you became a teacher. The process may suggest new connections between ideas and events that you may not have linked before.

For You

As you remember your teaching experiences, avoid asking yourself, "Let's see. What is something that happened to me as a teacher that was significant to my understanding of teaching?" Instead, read and think about each of the following nine cues, jotting down just enough words to remind you of the event that comes to mind.

- I recall:

1. A time I was surprised how one student responded to me...

_____

_____

_____

2. A time I was surprised how an entire class reacted...

_____

_____

_____

3. A class period that I wish had never happened...

_____

_____

_____

4. An incident that was my baptism of fire...

_____

_____

_____

5. The day I lost my innocence…

_____

_____

_____

6. A time I was forced to change…

_____

_____

_____

7. A time I felt a strong conflict between teaching and the rest of my life…

_____

_____

_____

8. A time I felt a strong connection between my teaching and the rest of my life…

_____

_____

_____

9. My best hour…

_____

_____

_____

Now go back. Look at each of those incidents. Which of these events taught you what teaching is really about? Choose one that gave you a significant insight, one you want to describe to others in your group. Write that story in some detail. (The events that you do not describe fully at this point are likely to be useful to you later with other strategies.)

_____

_____

_____

_____

_____

_____

_____

_____

_____

_____

_____

_____

_____

_____

For the Group	*Read your story* to your group. Tell the others the lesson about teaching that you learned from this incident. Ask them if there are other lessons a teacher might learn from this story. The purpose in your posing this question is not to find out if you interpreted the incident correctly. You did. The purpose of having others analyze this event is for you to have the opportunity to see the incident from another angle.

Strategy 2-4 **SIGNIFICANT** **TEACHERS**	This strategy is designed to help you see how your traits compare with those of significant teachers in your past.

For You	*In the "Name"* column of Figures 2.2 and 2.3, write the name of a teacher who comes to mind when you read each description. Do not repeat any teacher's name on these lists.

Remember a characteristic of the first teacher on the positively significant teacher list (Figure 2.2). If you have that same characteristic, list it in the center column ("Like me"). If you are different, write the characteristic in the right column ("Unlike me"). Think of more traits of this teacher and record each trait in the appropriate column. Include even those traits that may not seem relevant to teaching. Do the same for the rest of the teachers in Figure 2.2 and for each teacher in Figure 2.3.

Note whether some characteristics are repeated in the "Like me" column in each figure. Also, are any repeated in the "Unlike me" column?

For the Group	Report to the group ways you are like and unlike teachers who were both positively and negatively significant in your schooling. You might do that on a framework like the one shown in Figure 2.4.

Identify the characteristics that are uniquely yours. You might do this by (1) asking the group to identify the characteristics in your table that make you unique among the group or (2) doing the same analysis for yourself. You might also identify for the group the characteristics listed that you would prefer not be there.

Strategy 2-5 **REPGRIDDING** **YOUR TEACHERS**	In this strategy you will identify constructs that you use when describing teachers.

FIGURE 2.2: POSITIVELY SIGNIFICANT TEACHERS

A teacher who:	Name	Like me	Unlike me
I remember with fondness			
Had personal strength			
Really woke me up			
I would like to be like			
Changed me as a person			

FIGURE 2.3: NEGATIVELY SIGNIFICANT TEACHERS

A teacher who:	Name	Like me	Unlike me
I remember with displeasure			
Was very weak			
Wanted me to go through life with closed eyes			
Many kids liked, but I sure did not			
Is not yet on this list, but must be			

FIGURE 2.4: HOW MY TRAITS COMPARE WITH SOME OF MY PAST TEACHERS' TRAITS

	Like me	Unlike me
Positively significant teachers	1. 2. 3. 4.	1. 2. 3. 4.
Negatively significant teachers	1. 2. 3. 4.	1. 2. 3. 4.

For You   In the 1950s, George Kelly developed a theory of psychology, which he called personal construct theory (Kelly, 1955). The theory holds that each person sees the world in a unique way because everyone has a unique set of beliefs, that is, constructs. The particular set of constructs one has determines how that person experiences the environment.

Each of us has a set of constructs about schools, teaching, teachers, content areas, parents, and students. Kelly developed several techniques for identifying these constructs. He called one of these techniques the Repertory Grid. Over the years, researchers have developed many versions of the Repertory Grid, a term that is sometimes shortened to RepGrid. Several forms of the RepGrid are used in this book.

At the tops of the columns in Figure 2.5, write the names of any seven of the ten teachers identified in Strategy 2-4. Include the name of the teacher who you would "like to be like."

Note the three checks in the first row. Which two of the three teachers identified by the checks are most alike in their teaching? Circle their checks. How are the two teachers alike? Describe the similarity in a word or phrase, and record it in the right-hand column of the table under the word *Alike*.

How does the third teacher differ from the other two? Write a word or phrase describing this difference in the left-hand column under the word *Different*.

Note the three checks in the second row. Which two of the three teachers identified by these checks are most alike in their teaching? Describe this similarity, and enter the description in the right-hand column. Identify how the third teacher differs, and enter this difference in the left-hand column of row two. Continue comparing those teachers identified by the checks in the remaining six rows. Write their similarities and differences in the appropriate columns.

The words you have written in the right- and left-hand columns are some of your constructs about teachers. When you think of teachers, you think of them in these terms. These constructs are among those you use to create your image of teachers.

For the Group   *Compare your list* of constructs (constructs only, not the entire table) with those of other members of your group.

Identify any patterns or clusters in the constructs of others. For example, are several constructs in another list descriptive of a particular aspect of teaching?

Determine whether some lists are similar to others. Whose lists are most similar? Whose is most different from the others?

Different   Me   Alike

Difference Totals

Strategy 2-6
PATTERNS IN YOUR
REPGRID

This strategy, which builds upon the preceding one, uses your constructs of teaching to further describe you and others as teachers. *Note: To use this strategy most effectively, you must first complete Strategy 2-5.*

For You

Think of each of the eight pairs of constructs that you identified in Strategy 2-5 as opposite ends on a 0 to 3 continuum. You could describe each teacher on this scale by giving that teacher a number as follows:

- 0 = much like the left-hand construct
- 1 = somewhat like the left-hand construct
- 2 = somewhat like the right-hand construct
- 3 = much like the right-hand construct

With your completed RepGrid (Figure 2.5), note which two teachers you described as alike in the first row (they have circled checks under their names). Since you chose the construct on the right to describe them, they should get a rating of 3. Write a 3 in the space above the diagonal line in the first row in the same spaces as the circled checks.

Now rate each of the other five teachers and yourself on these two constructs by writing 0, 1, 2, or 3 in the space above the diagonal line in the first row under each of their names.

Repeat the two steps above with the other seven pairs of constructs.

Study the numbers in each teacher's column. Which pair of teachers has the most similar pattern of numbers? According to the constructs that you have identified, you have described these teachers as most alike. Do you agree with what this RepGrid shows? If you believe these two teachers are different in ways not identified on this RepGrid, then you have detected the presence of some new constructs that you use to describe teachers.

For the Group

Report the results of your RepGrid to the group. Are any of the results surprising? Describe the changes that you would have to make to become more like the teacher who you would "like to be like."

Strategy 2-7
QUANTIFYING YOUR
REPGRID

This strategy allows you to use the RepGrid to assign another set of numbers to yourself and the other seven teachers. The additional quantification will reveal the similarities and differences between yourself and other teachers. *Note: To use this strategy most effectively, you must first complete Strategy 2-6.*

For You   *Compare the number* you gave yourself with the numbers you gave the other teachers on the first pair of constructs in Figure 2.5. For all teachers with the same number as you, write a 0 to the right of the diagonal under their names. The 0 represents the difference between your rating and theirs. For those teachers with a rating of one more or one less than yours, write in a 1 under each name. Do not use plus or minus signs. In the same manner, write in 2s and 3s, if applicable, and then enter the difference numbers for the other seven pairs of constructs.

Total the difference numbers at the bottom of each column. Note that you are to add only the eight numbers that are to the right of the diagonals.

If any of the other teachers has a difference total of 0, it is because you gave that teacher the same ratings as you gave yourself. In other words, you described that teacher as being the same as you, according to the constructs that you identified. By contrast, you regard the teachers with the highest totals as most different from you.

Complete the following sentences:

I described _____ as a teacher with a low difference score, and I am pleased to see that teacher as similar to myself because

_____

_____.

But it is also important to me that I see myself as different from that teacher in this way:

_____

_____.

For the Group   *Read the sentences* that you completed to the group. Can your group identify any patterns in the ways that you all would like to differ from the teachers you described?

Strategy 2-8
EXTENDING
TEACHER REPGRIDS
    This strategy will help you to identify additional constructs that you use in describing teaching and to reveal similarities between yourself and other teachers. *Note: To use this strategy most effectively, you must first complete Strategy 2-5.*

Different   Me   Alike

Difference Totals

For You or the Group   *Complete the RepGrid* shown in Figure 2.6 using other groups of teachers, such as:

- other teachers in your school,
- fictional teachers, or
- your group members.

Strategy 2-9
SIGNIFICANT OTHERS   This strategy is designed to give you data for comparing some of your academic values with the values of those who were significant influences in your past.

For You   *In the left-hand* column of Figure 2.7, rows 2 to 5, enter the names of four people outside of school who were significant influences on you when you were growing up. Consider including parents, siblings, other relatives, peers, heroes, and religious leaders.

Rate yourself as you are now, recording the number above the diagonal, on a scale of 1-10, with 10 being high, on each of the following characteristics:

- skilled
- well-read
- schooled
- educated
- inquiring
- intelligent

FIGURE 2.7: ACADEMIC VALUES OF SIGNIFICANT OTHERS

Name	Skilled	Well-read	Schooled	Educated	Inquiring	Intelligent	Difference
Me	O	O	O	O	O	O	O

Rate the other people listed in the same way that you rated yourself. Below the diagonals, record the difference between each person's ratings and yours. Record all differences as positive numbers.

Sum the differences and record the sum in the last column. Determine who is most like you in the six characteristics. Who is most different? Do any of the results surprise you?

For the Group   Using this information, prepare and present to your group a brief statement about the influence of significant others on your academic values.

Strategy 2-10
WRITING YOUR
AUTOBIOGRAPHY

This strategy presents a way to write an autobiography of your teaching. Such a memoir can help you gain insight into why you teach as you do.

For You   *Look over the* events and stories that you recalled in Strategies 2-1, 2-2, and 2-3. As you prepare to write, bear in mind that an autobiography is more than a scrapbook of discontinuous vignettes. A good autobiography has a plot or theme. Therefore, you should search your stories for a recurring idea or image that illuminates the story of your teaching. As you pursue this theme, other relevant stories may come to mind, further developing the narrative.

Your autobiography might follow the development of a particular ideal or flaw. It might even build to a crisis and describe the resolution of that crisis. Or is your past a growing process? If so, what has grown? Or has it been a struggle? If so, between what forces? Has teaching revealed new aspects of you? If so, what are the new parts? Is the overall image one of building, sculpting, or evolution? What is it that carries you from day to day and year to year?

You are likely to want to describe only politically correct thoughts and feelings. Resist that temptation. What you thought and felt in the past is in the past. It is not necessarily what you think and feel now. Furthermore, honesty about the past is helpful in understanding the present. You need not, however, reveal thoughts and feelings you would be uncomfortable in sharing with your group. Perhaps your best choice is to select a theme and supporting stories with which you can be fully open.

Choose several of the events and stories that seem to hang together around a theme. Use them to write your autobiography as a teacher. Write out the stories in some detail, for it is the details that will help your readers relate your experiences to theirs. Also, in addition to factual information, describe the feelings and thoughts that you had at the time.

Think of your autobiography as information that can help you and others understand why you choose to teach the way you do. Your past did not force you to be what you are today. While you did not choose your family and probably had little choice over most of your educational experiences, you did have a choice about how you reacted to these situations. You also have choices about how you are going to respond in the future.

For the Group   Share your autobiography with your group members. Note the questions they ask. Then revise your autobiography to address the questions raised. Share any substantive additions with your group.

Strategy 2-11
I Used to Be a
Teacher Who...   This strategy directs you to recall past changes in your actions, thoughts, and feelings and to identify the changes that you would like to make in the future.

For You   *Complete the following* sentences by adding endings that:

• For 1-3, describe observable, related actions.

1. I used to be a teacher who...

_____

_____

_____

2. I am now a teacher who...

_____

_____

_____

3. I want to be a teacher who...

_____

_____

_____

• For 4-6, describe beliefs.

4. I used to be a teacher who believed that...

_____

_____

_____

5. I am now a teacher who believes that...

_____

_____

_____

6. I want to be a teacher who believes that...

_____

_____

_____

• For 7-9, identify feelings. Note that people often use the word *feel* to mean *believe*. What is wanted here is emotions rather than thoughts.

7. I used to be a teacher who had feelings of...

_____

_____

_____

8. I am now a teacher who has feelings of...

_____

_____

_____

9. I want to be a teacher who has feelings of...

_____

_____

_____

For the Group   *Each member of* your group could read a set of sentences and ask who else in the group acts, believes, or feels the same way. Or members of the group could write their sentences on 3" x 5" cards, have one set of three sentences read to the group, and have the group attempt to identify the author.

References   Kelly, George. 1955. *Psychology of Personal Constructs*. London: Norton.

CHAPTER 3

EXAMINING CURRENT TEACHING

The strategies in Chapter 2 explored your past to help you understand why you make the choices that you make now. This chapter will present 15 strategies to heighten your awareness of what you are doing now. Such awareness can immediately help you to make better-informed choices.

Strategy 3-1
JOURNALS
TO RECORD
WHAT I DO

With this strategy, you explore various types of journals, identify techniques that you can use in writing one, and begin keeping a journal.

Keeping a journal in order to understand the choices one makes is a widely known and effective technique. By allowing us to look closely at our experiences, journals can give us a window to view who we are and what we need.

Journal keeping is such a personal endeavor that setting specific guidelines might hinder the process rather than help it. Instead, some suggestions about journal writing will be presented. Consider them all, and try some of them.

A journal will be of maximum value to you if you do two things. First, record your true thoughts and feelings about your work as a teacher. It follows that the one best audience for your journal writing efforts is you. If you keep a journal that is read by a professor or by members of your group, you will be writing for them. You must be the sole audience if your journal is to reflect exactly who you are. Therefore, when you write, do so with the intention of never showing or reading your journal to anyone.

Second, make journal entries on a regular basis. Daily entries to the journal are not necessary, but writing only during times of crises will (one hopes) be too infrequent. Some find that it works to set particular times aside for writing (such as after dinner on Monday, Wednesday, and Friday).

However often you choose to write, you are most likely to write regularly if you develop some ways to discipline or reward yourself for making entries. One way to make the writing process a pleasant experience is to choose the journal with some care. Do you feel most comfortable writing on loose-leaf pages, in an easy-to-carry, pocket-sized spiral notebook, on a computer, in a diary with a lock on it, or in a book with blank pages bound between hand-tooled leather covers? Would the journal carry a special meaning if you decorated its cover with a photograph, a drawing of your own, or a picture cut from a greeting card or a magazine? Would you be more apt to make entries if you wrote with a pen used solely for that purpose, perhaps a real fountain pen, a pen with colored ink, or a pencil with a multicolor lead? Would the process be more pleasurable if you wrote only when you were in a special place set aside for writing?

For You   *Consider several forms* for the structure of your entries. Choose one or a variety of forms that makes writing fun and meaningful for you.

- *Letter to yourself.* Write the entry as a letter from the present you to a future you.

- *Unsent letter.* Write a letter that you would never send. Tell a student, parent, fellow teacher, or administrator your exact thoughts and feelings. An unsent letter can help you realize what you really believe and what you really want.

- *Feeling focus.* Begin the entry with a report of intense feelings you have at that moment or had earlier in the day. Do not ascribe any causes for these feelings, but do try for a full accounting of all the mixed feelings you experienced. Include the primary and secondary feelings, the overt and the subtle, and the pleasurable and aggravating. After you have completely described your feelings, write a dispassionate account of the events that preceded this moment of intense feeling. End your entry at this point without connecting the events with the feelings. You might want to leave a blank space in your journal, so that at a future time, you can enter an evaluation of this emotional moment.

- *Snapshot.* Record significant moments. Do not limit your choices to problems. Include incidents that seem to jump out. As soon as possible after the event, jot down key words that will help you remember what happened. Later, describe the event in your journal in some detail. First, describe what happened. Then explain what it means.

- *Conversation.* Frame the entry to take the form of a script recording a conversation between yourself and another person, or between your different selves, rational and emotional, free and restrained, or teacher and parent.

- *Insight notes.* Begin your sentences with phrases like "I wonder if..." "Could it be that..." "I noticed..." or "It seems to me that..."

- *Free writing.* Start with a topic and let the writing flow. Do not stop or be concerned whether what you write makes sense. Just let thoughts and feelings pop into your head and immediately out of the pen. Stop in the middle of a sentence and start another if ideas are pressingly urgent. (This kind of writing is not as easy as it sounds. It takes a certain level of discipline not to criticize yourself.)

For the Group   A journal can remain private and still benefit your group since your journal writing can facilitate insights into your teaching and into the work of the group.

You can support each other's journal writing by taking several minutes at each meeting to exchange your writing experiences. Talk about the successes you are having. Describe the types of writing you find particularly useful. Identify techniques that work in getting you to make regular entries.

Your group may agree that each of you will keep a record of personal events and that you will share these stories among yourselves. This type of writing is different from private journal writing. The emphasis is on reporting what group members do, rather than on what each believes and feels. Recording and reporting your stories can be very helpful to all of you, but think of that process as distinct from journal writing.

Strategy 3-2
CONTINUUM OF   This strategy includes techniques to clarify your feelings of professional com-
COMPETENCE   petence.

For You   *What events associated* with your teaching come to mind when you think of the word *competent?* On the number line in Figure 3.1, write several words that describe those events above the number 10. If no events readily come to mind, close your eyes and let yourself feel a sense of competence. Holding that feeling, let your mind run back and begin recalling teaching events. Which of these events do you associate with feelings of competence?

Now imagine yourself feeling inept. Recall a teaching experience that you associate with that feeling. Write a few words above the 0 on the continuum to identify that experience. If events in which you felt somewhat competent or mostly inept come to mind, add those in the appropriate places on the continuum.

Besides events, you can add the names of individuals or groups of people to the line. What level of competence do you feel when you are with students? If you can assign a number value to that, add the word *students* above that position on the line. Perhaps you can do the same for *bright students* and for *slow students.*

Figure 3.1: Continuum of Competence

Inept 0 1 2 3 4 5 6 7 8 9 10 Competent

Continue making additions to the line as you read this list:

- In the presence of students:

    1. with discipline problems

    2. with physical disabilities

    3. with emotional problems

    4. of the _____ ethnic group (specify)

    5. who are male

    6. who are female

    7. of a particular age (specify)

    8. such as _____ (name particular students)

    9. who are _____ (specify other types of students)

- In the presence of administrators:

    1. in general

    2. who are male

    3. who are female

    4. who are _____ (identify other)

- In the presence of parents (identify individuals and types)
- In the presence of supervisors
- In the presence of _____ (identify colleagues)
- In the presence of _____ (identify staff persons and positions)

- At certain times of the:

  1. day

  2. grading period

  3. year

- While performing these tasks:

  1. designing units

  2. writing tests

  3. grading tests

  4. introducing new material

  5. reviewing material

  6. conducting labs

  7. teaching _____ (specify subjects)

  8. coaching

  9. supervising extracurricular activities

- In certain places:

  1. classroom

  2. teachers' lounge

  3. hall

  4. administrative offices

Using the information you entered on the continuum, complete this sentence:

• I feel most competent when...

_____

_____

_____.

Now complete the sentence again using about half as many words by combining some items:

• I feel most competent when...

_____

_____.

Complete this sentence, filling in the type of information described in parentheses:

• I feel my most competent at *(time of day or year)*

_____

_____

when I am in *(names of places)*

_____

_____

with *(names of individuals or groups of people)*

_____

_____

doing *(list activities)*

_____

_____.

Complete this sentence, filling in the type of information described in parentheses:

- I feel most inept at *(time of day or year)*

  _____

  _____

when I am in *(names of places)*

  _____

  _____

with *(names of individuals or groups of people)*

  _____

  _____

doing *(list activities)*

  _____

  _____.

For the Group *Present your competency* continuum to your group and share your completed sentences with them.

Strategy 3-3
Going Beyond
Teaching With
the Competence
Continuum

With this strategy you can compare the competence you feel while teaching with the competence you feel in other situations. *Note: To use this strategy most effectively, you must first complete Strategy 3-2.*

For You *To gain insights* into how the competence you feel while teaching compares to the competence you feel in your life outside the teaching profession, add nonteaching events, people, times, and places to your competency continuum. Extend the line above 10 and below 0, if necessary. Do any experiences outside of school give you greater feelings of competence than those you sense while teaching?

For the Group   *As a group* try to agree on a statement that describes how the feelings of competence you all have about teaching compare to the sense of competence you all have outside of school.

Strategy 3-4
GRAPHS AND
MAPS

This strategy suggests graphic ways to represent your feelings of competence as they change in time and space. *Note: To use this strategy most effectively, you must first complete Strategy 3-2.*

For You   *On the graphs* shown in Figures 3.2 and 3.3, map the relationship between your feelings of competence and the different times of the day and year.

To gain some additional insights, indicate on a map of your school the areas where you feel the most and least competent.

For the Group   *Discuss the similarities* and contrasts that are evident in the periods and places of the highest and lowest feelings of competence.

Strategy 3-5
DESCRIBING
OTHER FEELINGS

This strategy suggests other professional feelings that you can investigate. *Note: To use this strategy most effectively, you must first complete Strategies 3-2, 3-3, and 3-4.*

For You   *Recalling your experiences* with the three preceding strategies, decide if you would find it worthwhile to apply any of those strategies to the following pairs of feelings.

- out of control versus in control

- discouraged versus enthusiastic

- angry versus serene

- dictated to versus free

- oblivious versus intensely aware

For the Group   *As a group*, discuss using the foregoing strategies to investigate new areas of professional feelings.

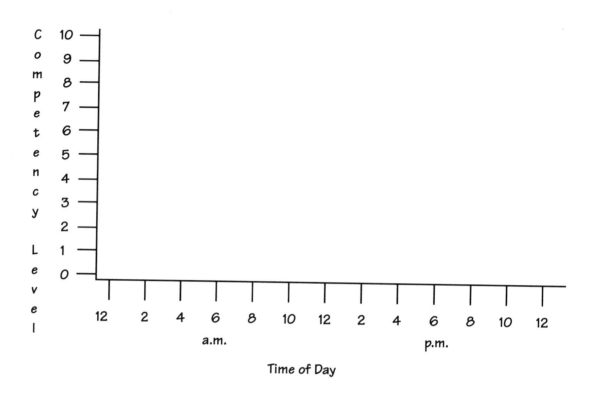

FIGURE 3.2: FEELINGS OF COMPETENCE AND TIME OF DAY

Time of Day

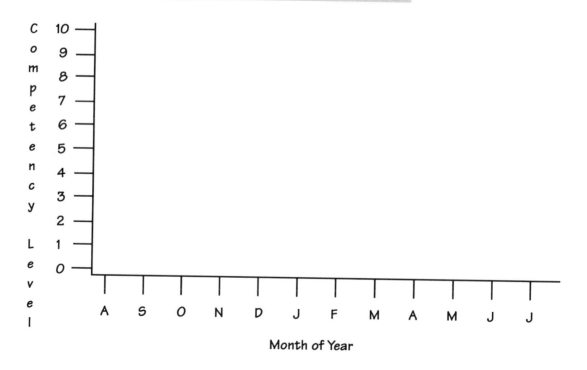

FIGURE 3.3: FEELINGS OF COMPETENCE AND TIME OF YEAR

Month of Year

Strategy 3-6
IT IS WITH
MIXED FEELINGS

With this strategy, you focus on a set of feelings that you experience while teaching and consider the effect of those feelings on your behavior.

For You

Watch for a time in the next week when you experience some intense feelings in response to some teaching-related occurrence. List the feelings (preferably while you are still experiencing them), but do not attribute causes to them. Try to identify all of your feelings, remembering that while one or two feelings generally dominate at emotional times, more subtle feelings are usually present as well. Use words such as:

lost	confused	relieved	betrayed
angry	frustrated	competent	aggressive
incomplete	determined	stimulated	powerless
warm	joyous	pleased	cold
loved	hated	rejected	ecstatic
accepted	closed	courageous	discouraged
controlled	peaceful	aware	fragmented

Write a dispassionate account of the event that brought about these feelings. Concentrate on recording only the facts. Do not explain how these events brought about your feelings, and try to avoid using value-laden modifiers.

Ask yourself, would I want this mix of feelings to occur again? If the answer is yes, what can you do to bring about these feelings? If the answer is no, what can you do to avoid a recurrence? What might be gained if you changed your behavior in these ways? What would be lost?

For the Group

Ask a group member to read your account of the event to the entire group. Then you read the list of your emotions. You might ask the others what their reactions would have been. You might tell the others how you could change your behavior to bring about or to avoid these feelings. You may also wish to ask your colleagues what they think might be lost if you changed your behavior in the ways that you have described.

Strategy 3-7
REPGRIDDING
SOME STUDENTS

This strategy will help you identify some of the constructs (or sets of beliefs) that you use in describing students. You will use a variation of the Repertory Grid (RepGrid) developed by David Hunt (1980).

For You

Identify twelve students who fit the categories given below. (If you are not currently teaching, use the names of students in your recent past.) Record the names at the top of the columns in Figure 3.4. Do not use any student's name twice.

- At the top of the first column, write the name of one of your best male students.

- At the top of the second column, write the name of one of your weakest male students.

- At the top of the third column, write the name of a male student who has made great gains in your class.

- At the top of the fourth column, write the name of a male student whom you have not helped much.

- At the top of the fifth column, write the name of a male student you like.

- At the top of the sixth column, write the name of a male student you like less than most other students.

- At the top of columns seven through twelve, write the name of female students in the same categories: one of the best, one of the weakest, someone who has made great gains, someone you have not helped much, someone you like, and someone you like less than most.

Note the three checks in the first row. Which two of the three students identified by these checks (one of the best male students, a male student you have not helped much, and one of the weakest female students) are most alike? Circle the checks below their names. How are these two alike? Describe the similarity in a word or short phrase, and write the descriptor in the right-hand column of the figure under the word *Alike*. How is the third student different from the other two? Write the word or phrase describing the difference in the left-hand column of the figure under the word *Different*.

Repeat the foregoing procedure for the remaining eleven rows. Try to identify similarities and differences that you have not used before on the grid.

Examine the words that you have written in the right and left columns of Figure 3.4. These are some of the constructs that you use when you formulate an image of a student. Describe the relationships that you see among your constructs:

- Relationship 1—

_____

_____

_____

FIGURE 3.4: IDENTIFYING CONSTRUCTS ABOUT STUDENTS

Alike

Male Students: Best, Weakest, Gains, Few Gains, Like, Like Less

Female Students: Best, Weakest, Gains, Few Gains, Like, Like Less

Different

• Relationship 2—

_____

_____

_____

For the Group *Compare your list* of 24 constructs with those of other group members. Try to discern patterns, or clusters, in the sets of constructs used by other members. Also identify the lists that are most similar.

Strategy 3-8
PATTERNS IN
YOUR REPGRID

This strategy uses the constructs about students that you identified in Figure 3.4 to isolate some of the similarities that you see in students. *Note: To use this strategy most effectively, you must first complete Strategy 3-7.*

For You *Think of each* of your pairs of constructs as being on opposite ends of a 0 to 3 continuum. You will describe all students named in Figure 3.4 by giving each of them numbers as follows:

- 0 = much like the left-hand construct
- 1 = somewhat like the left-hand construct
- 2 = somewhat like the right-hand construct
- 3 = much like the right-hand construct

Note which two students in the first row are described as being alike (they have circled checks under their names). Since you chose the construct on the right to describe them, they should get a rating of 3. Write a 3 in the same spaces as the circled checks. The remaining student, who was described as different, will probably get a 0. Go on to rate each of the other nine students on these two constructs by writing a 0, 1, 2, or 3 under each of their names in the first row.

Use the 0-3 scale to describe the students on the other 11 pairs of constructs. Then look at the numbers in each student's column. Which pair of students has the most similar pattern of numbers? According to the constructs that you have identified, these students are the most alike. Do you agree with what the RepGrid shows? If you believe that these two students are different in ways not identified on this RepGrid, then you have detected some new constructs that you use to describe students.

For the Group   *Report the results* of this RepGrid to your group. Discuss how the constructs that you use could interfere with how you relate to some students.

Strategy 3-9
TYPES OF
INTELLIGENCE

This strategy is designed to help you identify how you use various types of intelligences to describe your students. *Note: To use this strategy most effectively, you must first complete Strategy 3-7.*

You can gain additional meaning from the RepGrid in Figure 3.4 by further classifying the data. Howard Gardner's types of intelligence provides one useful scheme for grouping teachers' constructs of students. Gardner, in *Frames of Mind* (1983), proposes that the word *intelligence* should be thought of in the plural. That is, people do not possess a single ability called intelligence, but instead have an array of intelligences, some more prominent than others. Gardner postulates at least seven facets of intelligence:

1. A person with strong *linguistic* intelligence is fluent in speech, enjoys writing, has a good memory for words and trivia, and thinks in words.

2. A person with strong *logical-mathematical* intelligence is logical, solves problems effectively, likes puzzles, and is inclined to experiment.

3. A person with strong *spatial* intelligence excels in visual arts and geometry and is inclined to design, draw, and build models.

4. A person with strong *musical* intelligence is rhythmical, is likely to sing or play an instrument, and enjoys music.

5. A person with strong *body-kinesthetic* intelligence is well-coordinated, physically at ease, comfortable handling objects, and creative in movement.

6. A person with strong *interpersonal* intelligence respects others, has multi-cultural understanding, is likely to be active in committees or clubs, and is cooperative, caring, friendly, and sociable.

7. A person with strong *intrapersonal* intelligence is self-confident, responsible, ethical, independent, self-motivating, and iconoclastic.

For You   *Classify your 24* constructs about students (from Figure 3.4) by the type of intelligence they require. Enter the constructs in the appropriate spaces in Figure 3.5. Some of your constructs may not fall within one of Gardner's types. Enter such constructs in the section labeled "Unclassified."

Using your data from Figure 3.5, complete the following sentence with the information indicated in parentheses:

• I am more apt to think of students in terms of their *(one or more of Gardner's*

*types of intelligences)*_____

_____ ability, than their

*(others of Gardner's types of intelligence)*_____

_____ ability.

For the Group   *Compare your sentence* with the sentences of others in your group. Determine whether you would want to think of students in terms of other abilities, and if so, how that might be done.

Strategy 3-10   This strategy can help you focus on the ways that you design instruction for
CHANGING   individual students. *Note: To use this strategy most effectively, you must first com-*
STUDENTS   *plete Strategy 3-7.*

For You   *In the left-hand* column of Figure 3.6 under "Student pair," write the names of the 12 pairs of students you have designated as alike (those with circled checks on the RepGrid shown in Figure 3.4).

With regard to the first pair of students, ask yourself, "What is one thing that I would like to accomplish with these two students?" Write your response in the second column under "Goal." Then ask the same question concerning the other 11 pairs of students and record your responses.

For each of the 12 pairs of students, ask yourself, "How would I work with these students to accomplish the goals that I identified?" Record your responses in the third column under "Teaching approach."

You have identified 12 teaching approaches, or interventions, from your teaching repertoire. Now use the scales in Figure 3.7 to identify some characteristics of these approaches. No judgment of goodness or badness is implied by the descriptors on these scales, regardless of whether answers fall on the left or right ends. You must decide whether the scales are valid ways of describing your approaches, and if so, whether you want to make any change in your instructional interventions because of this new information.

Types of intelligence	My constructs of students
Linguistic	
Logical-mathematical	
Spatial	
Musical	
Body-kinesthetic	
Interpersonal	
Intrapersonal	
Unclassified	

• Consider the teaching approach listed in row A of Figure 3.6. Answer the questions that follow about that approach, and record your answers by writing an A in the appropriate position on each scale in Figure 3.7.

1. To what degree does this approach allow student choice? If the intervention is designed by you and carried out by you without student feedback, the A would be written over the 0 on the left side of the scale. If each student has wide-ranging choice, the A would be written above the 4.

2. To what extent does this intervention deal directly with what you want to accomplish? If, for example, you want to help students be more forceful when delivering an oral presentation, a direct approach would be to teach them about proper body position and eye contact. An indirect approach might be to work on developing self-confidence or on choosing topics of personal interest.

3. To what extent does this approach have each student work alone, rather than in collaboration with other students?

4. To what degree would you consider this technique to be innovative?

Student pair		Goal	Teaching approach	Construct
A	&			
B	&			
C	&			
D	&			
E	&			
F	&			
G	&			
H	&			
I	&			
J	&			
K	&			
L	&			

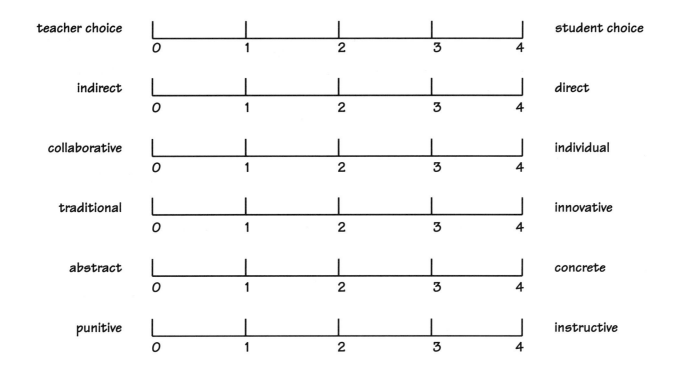

5. Is this intervention based on the concrete (observable, manipulative) or the abstract (conceptual, theoretical, verbal)?

6. Does this intervention punish the student for incorrect responses or behavior, or is it designed to provide instruction in how to exhibit the more appropriate response?

• Answer questions 1-6 above for each of the other 11 teaching approaches that you identified on Figure 3.6. Record your responses on the scales in Figure 3.7 by writing in the letters B through L.

Consider the distribution of letters A-L on the choice scale. Are the letters clustered together? If so, try to make a statement describing your teaching approaches relative to this dimension. If there are several clusters of letters, specify what the approaches in each cluster have in common. If the letters are scattered along the scale, your statement should interpret what that distribution means about the types of interventions you use in your teaching.

Examine the distribution of the letters on each of the other scales. Do you see any patterns? What do they reveal about your teaching approaches?

For the Group *Report the results* of this strategy to your group. You might want to duplicate Figures 3.6 and 3.7, reveal your insights about your teaching approaches to the group, and ask colleagues if they see any other patterns. Or you may elect to report only your conclusions.

Strategy 3-11
THEORETICAL BASES FOR TEACHING APPROACHES

This strategy can help you identify the theoretical rationales that determine your intervention strategy choices. *Note: To use this strategy most effectively, you must first complete Strategies 3-7 and 3-10.*

You will be asked to make some of your instructional theories explicit. The task may be difficult since you will be asked to look at your practices in order to identify their bases in theory. This sequence is the reverse of what is commonly done with theory and practice in education. Typically teachers are given theory and then are expected to develop practice based on the theory.

Here, however, you are not being asked to select practices in accord with someone else's theory. You are being encouraged to identify the theories that are in harmony with your own practices.

For You *Copy the constructs* from the "Alike" column in Figure 3.4 to the "Construct" column of Figure 3.6. The latter figure now lists 12 of your constructs about students, identifies a goal you have for students with each of these characteristics, and describes an approach that you would use with students with these characteristics.

Analyze your data to answer the following questions.

• What relationships do you see between your constructs, your goals, and your approaches?

• What was your reason for choosing the goals that you did for the students listed?

• Why did you choose the interventions that you did?

• Did you have a different set of reasons if you were working toward a cognitive goal rather than toward an affective one?

• Did you have a different rationale if you wanted to develop a student's strength rather than help the student overcome a weakness?

• Did your reasons differ according to the cognitive ability of the student? According to the developmental stage of the student? According to the student's emotional strength?

Develop a statement describing the theories that you use in selecting goals and teaching approaches. If you have difficulty formulating the statement, take your completed Figure 3.6 to your group, along with your preliminary thoughts, and ask your colleagues to help you put your statement together.

For the Group   *Discuss the statements* describing each group member's instructional theories.

Strategy 3-12
I Am the Kind
of Teacher
Who…

The purpose of this strategy is to raise your awareness of your professional thoughts and feelings. The original version of this strategy, which was developed by counselor and art teacher Rosemarie Schultz, is described in her book, *Journey to the Center of Your World* (1984).

For You   *On Figure 3.8*, record what you did during a five- to ten-minute period in your role as a teacher. You might, for instance, focus on what you DID this morning during the 5 to 10 minutes after you first saw the school building. Begin each sentence with the words, "I am the kind of teacher who…" For example:

- I am the kind of teacher who drives a Dodge minivan to school.

- I am the kind of teacher who looks for the same parking spot each day.

- I am the kind of teacher who is one of the first to get to school each day.

- I am the kind of teacher who double-checks to be sure the van is locked.

- I am the kind of teacher who carries into the building a large handbag that holds a novel, students' papers, an apple, some yogurt, and a grocery shopping list.

- I am the kind of teacher who tries to catch the eye of the students who are standing around outside so that I can say "Good morning" to them.

Next, and also on Figure 3.8, redescribe the same period by recording what you THOUGHT. For example:

- I am the kind of teacher who thinks that the van says more about me as a parent than about me as a teacher.

- I am the kind of teacher who thinks that having assigned parking spots would make getting to work a little easier every morning.

- I am the kind of teacher who thinks that it might not be safe to leave my child's library books in the van. Ditto the clothes I'm going to take to the cleaners after school.

- I am the kind of teacher who thinks that a little more parking lot security would make this job more attractive.

- I am the kind of teacher who thinks that it sometimes seems as though I have to carry my whole life around in this bag.

- I am the kind of teacher who thinks that these students need all the attention from caring adults that they can get.

Now redescribe the same period by writing down how you FELT. For example:

- I am the kind of teacher who feels like a parent when I drive this van.

- I am the kind of teacher who would like not to have to worry about finding a parking place.

- I am the kind of teacher who feels secure only if the van is safe during the day.

- I am the kind of teacher who feels concerned about my property.

- I am the kind of teacher who feels uneasy about having mixed school and home in this bag.

- I am the kind of teacher who feels wanted when students respond positively to me.

To gain more insight into the kind of teacher you are, answer the questions in Figure 3.9. Then, considering your responses in Figures 3.8 and 3.9, complete Figure 3.10 with any INSIGHTS you may have gained from this strategy. For example:

- I am the kind of teacher who feels stressed by the need to juggle home and school responsibilities.

- I am the kind of teacher who is concerned about convenience and material property.

- I am the kind of teacher who is willing to take a chance when it comes to my students.

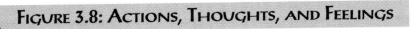

What you DID in five to ten minutes.

I am the kind of teacher who _____

_____

I am the kind of teacher who _____

_____

I am the kind of teacher who _____

_____

I am the kind of teacher who _____

_____

I am the kind of teacher who _____

_____

I am the kind of teacher who _____

_____

I am the kind of teacher who _____

_____

I am the kind of teacher who _____

_____

I am the kind of teacher who _____

_____

I am the kind of teacher who _____

_____

What you THOUGHT in the same period.

I am the kind of teacher who thinks _____

_____

I am the kind of teacher who thinks _____

_____

I am the kind of teacher who thinks _____

_____

I am the kind of teacher who thinks _____

_____

I am the kind of teacher who thinks _____

_____

I am the kind of teacher who thinks _____

_____

I am the kind of teacher who thinks _____

_____

I am the kind of teacher who thinks _____

_____

I am the kind of teacher who thinks _____

_____

I am the kind of teacher who thinks _____

_____

What you FELT in the same period.

I am the kind of teacher who feels _____

_____

I am the kind of teacher who feels _____

_____

I am the kind of teacher who feels _____

_____

I am the kind of teacher who feels _____

_____

I am the kind of teacher who feels _____

_____

I am the kind of teacher who feels _____

_____

I am the kind of teacher who feels _____

_____

I am the kind of teacher who feels _____

_____

I am the kind of teacher who feels _____

_____

I am the kind of teacher who feels _____

_____

FIGURE 3.9: MORE ABOUT ME

Which of the things I did, thought, and felt today were typical of me? _____

_____

_____

Which of these things were not like me? _____

_____

_____

To what degree am I taking care of

myself?	0	1	2	3	4	5	6	7	8	9	10
my students?	0	1	2	3	4	5	6	7	8	9	10
my friends and family?	0	1	2	3	4	5	6	7	8	9	10

Am I organized? ....yes.......mostly........somewhat.................no

Am I more accepting of or resistant to the tasks of the day?..................................... accepting........resistant

Are the feelings that I recorded about teaching more positive or more negative?...... positive...........negative

Are my feelings about my students more positive or negative? .... positive...........negative

About my co-workers?.. positive...........negative

About parents?... positive...........negative

About the administration? .... positive...........negative

Of all the statements I wrote, which ones do I most wish were different? _____

_____

_____

If the statements that I wrote were the description of another teacher, how would I feel about that person

as a teacher? _____

_____

_____

I'm the kind of teacher who _____

_____

_____

I'm the kind of teacher who _____

_____

_____

I'm the kind of teacher who _____

_____

_____

I'm the kind of teacher who _____

_____

_____

For the Group   *From Figure 3.10*, read your four variations of "I am the kind of teacher who..." to your group. Decide what kind of response you want from the group and announce your decision before you begin to read. Your directions could vary from "I would like you to listen and make no comments" to "I would like each of you to complete the following sentence in a way that I have not: '_____ is the kind of teacher who...' "

Strategy 3-13
TEACHING AS AN "F" WORD

This strategy may reveal some of your implicit thinking about teaching.

For You   *The list that* follows contains all of the more than five hundred words on the first 20 pages under the letter *F* in the New College Edition of *The American Heritage Dictionary of the English Language* (1975). Very few of these words are normally viewed as descriptive of the act of teaching. You may see any one of these words, however, as having some meaningful connection to your teaching. Read through the list and underline those words that are in any way descriptive of your teaching. Skip those words that have no meaning for you.

fable	facial	factotum	failing
fabliau	facies	factual	faille
fabric	facile	facula	fail-safe
fabricate	facilitate	facultative	failure
fabrication	facility	faculty	fain
fabulist	facing	fad	faineant
fabulous	facsimile	faddish	faint
facade	fact	fade	faint-hearted
face	fact-finding	fade-in	faints
face card	faction	fadeless	fair
face cloth	factious	fade-out	fair ball
face lifting	factitive	faena	fair catch
faceplate	factor	fag	fair copy
facet	factorable	fagot	Fair Deal
facetiae	factorial	Fahrenheit	fairground
facetious	factorize	faience	fair-haired
face value	factory	fail	fairing

fairish

fairlead

fairly

fair-minded

fair play

fair sex

fair shake

fair-spoken

fair-trade

fairway

fair-weather

fairy

fairyland

fairy ring

fairy tale

fait accompli

faith

faith cure

faithful

faith healer

faithless

fake

faker

fakir

falbala

falcate

falchion

falciform

falcon

falconer

falconet

falcon-gentle

falconry

faldstool

Faulkner

fall

fallacious

fallacy

fallal

fallen woman

fallfish

fall guy

fallible

falling-out

falling star

fall line

Fallopian tube

fall out

fallout

fallow

fallow crop

fallow deer

false

false alarm

false arrest

false bottom

false colors

false-hearted

falsehood

false imprison-ment

false indigo

false keel

false pretense

false rib

false Solomon's seal

false step

falsetto

falsework

falsies

falsify

falsity

Falstaffian

faltboat

falter

fame

familial

familiar

familiarity

familiarize

family

family name

family skeleton

family tree

famine

famish

famous

famulus

fan

fanatic

fanatical

fanaticism

fan belt

fancied

fancier

fanciful

fancy

fancy-free

fancywork

fandango

fanfare

fanfaronade

fang

fanlight

fan mail

fanny

fanon

fantail

fantan

fantasia

fantast

fantastic

fantasy

fantoccini

fan vaulting

fan window

fanwort

far

farad

faraday

faradic

farandole

faraway

farce

farceur

farcical

farcy

fardel

fare

Far East

farewell

farfetched

far-flung

farina

farinose

farm

farmer

farm hand

farmhouse

farmstead

farmyard

farnesol

faro

far-off

farouche

far-out

far point

farrago

far-reaching

farrier

farrow

farseeing

far-sighted

farther

farthermost

farthest

farthing

farthingale

fasces

fascia

fascicle

fasciculus

fascinate

fascination

fascine

fascism

fascist

fashion

fashionmonger

fashion plate

fast

fast day

fasten

fastening

fastidious

fastigate

fastness

fat

fatal

fatality

fatback

fat cat

fate

fated

fateful
Fates
fathead
father
father confessor
fatherhood
father-in-law
fatherland
fatherless
fatherly
Father's Day
fathom
Fathometer
fathomless
fatidic
fatigable
fatigue
Fatima
fatling
fat-soluble
fatten
fattish
fatty

fatty acid
fatuity
fatuous
fat-witted
faubourg
faucal
fauces
faucet
faugh
Faulkner
fault
faultfinder
faultless
fault plane
faulty
faun
fauna
Faust
fauteil
faux pas
fava bean
faveolate
favonian

favor
favorable
favored
favorite
favorite son
favoritism
favus
Fawkes
fawn
fawn lily
fay
fayalite
faze
fazenda
FBI
FCC
FDA
FDIC
FDR
Fe
fealty
fear
fearful

fearless
fearnaught
fearsome
feasance
feasible
feast
Feast of Dedication
Feast of Lanterns
Feast of Lights
feat feather
feather bed
featherbed
featherbone
featherbrain
feathered
featheredge
feather grass
featherhead
feather palm
feather star
featherstitch
feather-veined
featherweight

feathery

feature

feature-length

febricity

febrifacient

febrific

febrifuge

febrile

February

fecal

feces

feckless

feculent

fecund

fecundate

fecundity

fed

federacy

federal

federalism

federalist

Federalist Party

federalize

federate

federation

federative

fedora

fee

feeble

feeble-minded

feed

feedback

feedbag

feeder

feeder line

feel

feeler

feeling

fee simple

fee splitting

feet

fee tail

feeze

feign

feint

feint-hearted

feist

feisty

feldspar

felicific

felicitate

felicitation

felicitous

felicity

feline

fell

fellow

fellow feeling

fellow man

fellow servant

fellowship

fellow traveler

felly

felon

felonious

felonry

felony

felony murder

felsite

felt

felting

felucca

fenwort

female

feme sole

feminine

feminine ending

feminine rhyme

femininity

feminism

feminize

femme fatale

femoral

femur

fen

fenagle

fence

fencer

fencing

fend

fender

fenestra

fenestrated	ferny	ferrous sulfate	festival
fennec	ferocious	ferruginous	festivity
fennel	ferocity	ferrule	festoon
fanny	ferret	ferry	festschrift
fenugreek	ferriage	ferryboat	fetal
feoff	ferric	ferryman	fetation
feral	ferric oxide	fertile	fetch
Ferber	ferricyanic acid	Fertile Crescent	fetching
fer-de-lance	ferricyanide	fertility	fete
fere	ferriferous	fertilization	feticide
feretory	Ferris wheel	fertilize	fetid
feria	ferrite	fertilizer	fetish
farine	ferroalloy	ferula	fetishism
ferity	ferroconcrete	ferule	fetlock
fermata	ferroelectric	fervency	fetor
ferment	ferromagnetism	fervent	fetter
fermentation	ferromagnet	fervid	fetterbush
fermative	ferromagnetic	fervor	fettle
Fermi	ferromanganese	fescue	fettling
fermion	ferrosilicon	fess	fetus
fermium	ferrotype	fess point	feud
fernery	ferrous	festal	feudal
fern seed	ferrous oxide	fester	feudalism

feudalize	fever blister	feverweed	Feynman
feudatory	feverfew	feverwort	fez
feudist	feverish	few	
fever	fever tree	fey	

Look over your list of words and group those together that are similar in the way they describe your teaching. What insights about the nature of your teaching did you gain from your consideration of this list of words?

For the Group   *Report to the* group whatever insights you gained about your teaching from this strategy. Duplicate your list of meaningful words and ask if anyone sees any different patterns.

Strategy 3-14
I USED TO BE A
TEACHER WHO…   This strategy can help you to reconsider former responses in light of the new insights you have gained from the strategies in this chapter. *Note: To use this strategy most effectively, you must first complete Strategy 2-11.*

For You   *Review your responses* from Strategy 2-11 to see if you would change any of them now.

For the Group   *Members of the* group could each describe one significant difference in their responses to Strategy 2-11 and this one.

Strategy 3-15
WHY I AM
DOING THIS   This strategy is to help you to identify the factors that influence you as you make professional choices and to identify new types of choices that you would like to make.

For You   *In response to* the cues that follow, describe who you are as a teacher, why you are that way, and what you might do differently. Limit yourself to several facets of yourself. Also, do not denigrate yourself. If you do, you are likely to feel guilty and to excuse rather than understand yourself. Focus instead on writing positive, nonjudgmental statements.

• Who I am as a teacher—

_____

_____

_____

• Why I am the way that I am as a teacher—

_____

_____

_____

• What I might do differently—

_____

_____

_____

For the Group   *Tell the group* your responses to the preceding cues. Relate only those insights that you have formed since you began meeting with your group. Make only positive, uncritical statements about yourself.

References   *A New College Edition of the American Heritage Dictionary of the English Language.* 1975. Boston: Houghton Mifflin.

Gardner, Howard. 1983. *Frames of Mind.* New York: Basic Books.

Hunt, David. 1980. "How to Be Your Own Best Theorist," *Theory into Practice,* 19(4): 287–293.

Schultz, Rosemarie. 1984. *Journey to the Center of Your World.* Englewood Cliffs, N.J.: Prentice Hall.

CHAPTER 4

READING YOUR METAPHORS

When you make decisions and act on them, you usually do not verbalize the theories on which your thinking and actions are based. What's more, even though your actions are a result of your beliefs, you are often not aware of the beliefs that prompt your actions.

There is a way, however, to reveal your beliefs. It involves looking at the words that you use when you describe what you do. These words will often be in the form of metaphor.

Many people see metaphor simply as a technique that writers use to make language interesting. Although they may value metaphor for its fascinating imagery, they are likely to see it as more of a hindrance than an aid to logical thought. Clear communication, they would insist, demands clear, clean, denotative language—words that stand alone with their own definite meaning.

But language is not so simple. In fact, the image-rich, connotative language that we use can tell us a great deal about our logic.

George Lakoff and Mark Johnson are among those who insist that metaphor cannot be relegated to the periphery of thought. In their 1980 book, *Metaphors We Live By*, Lakoff and Johnson clearly show that metaphor is central to what we perceive, think, and do.

Lakoff and Johnson define metaphor as "understanding and experiencing one kind of thing in terms of another." This definition of metaphor includes well-known implied comparisons:

- the simile, as in *A teacher is like a factory supervisor.*
- the analogy, as in *Both schools and factories take raw materials and refine them into increasingly finished products.*
- the traditional metaphor, as in *Our principal is nothing but a factory manager.*

The Lakoff and Johnson definition also encompasses, however, the subtle use of metaphor in comments such as:

- He went back to school to *retool* his skills.
- This class is about the *rawest material* that I have ever seen.

- Her class has little *down time*.
- We all strived for *zero reject* this year.
- Let's be good *workers* today.
- You can take a *break* when you finish the *job*.
- She can *crank out* a 500-word paper in no time.
- That high school *produced a fine batch* of graduates this year.

The metaphors used in such sentences reveal that the authors of the sentences understand and experience some things (schools) in terms of something else (factories).

The metaphors that we choose are highly significant because the influence of metaphor goes far beyond the words used to describe concepts. In fact, metaphor determines how we define the concept itself.

To show how metaphor determines our thoughts and actions about a concept, Lakoff and Johnson use the example of how we understand and experience the concept of argument in terms of war. If, metaphorically, argument is war, then the words that we use to speak about argument are likely to include phrases like *fought it out, shot him down, attacked, the right strategy, gain ground, win and lose,* and *on target.*

These words are more than descriptions. They identify the essence of the act of arguing. That essence is warlike. We fight it out. We attack the other party. We develop strategy. We shoot down positions. We battle to win.

Imagine, instead, that we experienced argument as a ballroom dance. Viewing argument as dance would result in very different language and actions. When talking about argument, we would use words like *partners, whirled, rhythm, in step,* and *glided.* If argument were dance, imagine how graciously you might start an argument. Consider how civilly you might behave during an argument. Think of how satisfactorily an argument might end.

Typically, though, when learning the concept of argument, we learn to see it as a war. We describe argument in terms of war because that is what it is to us. The metaphorical concept of "argument is war" is so central to our understanding of argument that "argument as dance" would not be recognizable to us.

Metaphors in Education   The passages that follow are comments that two teachers might make to their colleagues in the lounge at the end of a good day. The two teachers see similar problems with their classes, respond in similar ways, and achieve similar results. As you read what they say, note these similarities, but also try to detect the differences in the words used.

Teacher Pitcher: I don't get a day like this very often. Sometimes it's difficult to get the idea of photosynthesis across to these students, but today's class caught it pretty quickly. Maybe my little lecture to them yesterday helped some. They were just not very alert. I told them that they were not likely to catch much unless they paid more attention. They couldn't just sit there and expect things to soak in. Michael threw it back to me. He thought my comments were unfair. He said the class was getting more than I thought. I told him he might be right, but unless they put things into their own words, I don't really know what they've got. From the flow of give and take we had today, I think he may be right. Maybe my ideas were coming across more clearly than I thought.

Teacher Pointer: I don't get a day like this very often. Sometimes it's hard for these students to grasp photosynthesis, but this class picked it up pretty quickly. Maybe my little lecture to them yesterday helped some. They were passive and just were not responding as I expected. I told them that they were not likely to learn much unless they became more active. They had to dig in and uncover these concepts for themselves. Michael said that he found my comments unfair. The class was finding more than I thought. I told him that he might be right, but they shouldn't always leave it up to me to pull it out of them. Unless they give it back, I don't really know what they're picking up. From the way things went today, maybe he was right. Maybe they have been coming up with more than I thought.

In the scripts of the two teachers, you can pick out the words in each passage that reveal the nature of the metaphor for learning held by each teacher. Words such as *find*, *get*, *catch*, *things*, and *it* reveal that both Pitcher and Pointer hold the metaphor *knowledge is an object*. But they also believe that for learning to occur a student must come into possession of this object. In short, they think that knowing is possessing items of knowledge.

Pitcher and Pointer's ideas differ, however, about the role the teacher plays in causing students to possess knowledge. Pitcher sees the process as beginning with the teacher's "idea of photosynthesis." This idea is put into words that "get the idea ... across" to the students. The students "catch" the words, translate them into "their own words" and "give" them back to the teacher to provide evidence of "what they've got." A good lesson consists of a smooth "flow" of such "give and take."

Unlike Pitcher, Pointer does not directly transfer knowledge. Instead, the students must "dig in," "uncover" the knowledge, and "pick it up." To find out what these students have "come up with," Pointer could "pull it out" of them, but prefers to be less active and have the students just "give it back."

Thus, Pointer and Pitcher hold the same metaphors for knowledge and for learning. Pointer, however, has a different metaphor for the role of the teacher. To Pointer, a teacher is a guide who aids students in finding objects of knowledge, rather than the source of the objects themselves.

These teachers do not merely use different words to describe similar experiences. They operate according to different theories of learning, and they act differently because they have differing concepts of what it means to teach. They experience teaching in different ways and express their experiences with different metaphors.

Although both Pitcher and Pointer took Theories of Learning in graduate school, they did not develop their theories about teaching and learning from that course. Pitcher and Pointer formed their theories from their own experiences.

Even so, it is unlikely that Pitcher and Pointer could describe their theories. They are not even consciously aware of what these ideas are. They could, however, become more knowledgeable about their concepts by paying attention to the words they use when talking about teaching. And so can you.

The revelations that you can get from examining the metaphors that you use are not limited to your concepts of knowledge, learning, and role as a teacher. You understand and experience all aspects of your professional world in terms of other things. You have metaphors for your classroom, students, school, administrators, and the subjects that you teach.

Strategies 4-1 through 4-10 will help you identify the metaphors that you use to guide your teaching. Being aware of these metaphors can benefit you in three ways:

1. You can evaluate the effects of your metaphors on your practice (also see Strategies 4-11 to 4-13).

2. You can better evaluate how new teaching approaches fit with your current concepts. Strategy 4-14 shows how to evaluate the potential usefulness of materials by identifying their metaphors.

3. By changing a single metaphor, you can significantly alter a variety of your teaching behaviors, according to the work of Kenneth Tobin (1990) at Florida State University. Tobin believes that instead of changing the way you act as a teacher by identifying specific behaviors and attempting to change these behaviors, you could select a new metaphor and act from that metaphor. As a result, you would change a series of behaviors, including some you have not even identified. Changing your teaching by changing your metaphors would make a valuable teacher-based action research project as described in the last chapters of this book.

Strategy 4-1

SEARCHING FOR
YOUR METAPHORS
OF TEACHING

This strategy helps you find clues to the metaphors that you use to describe your teaching. *Note: To use this strategy effectively, you must first complete Strategy 2-1.*

For You

In general, teaching can be described as an act of transferring knowledge, of covering material, or of establishing a process. Verbs used to describe the transferring of knowledge include:

advise	convey	give	notify	tell
apprise	deliver	hand to	put over	transfer
communicate	get across	inform	recommend	transmit

Some verbs used to describe the coverage of material are:

complete	end	go back	stop
conclude	finish	go over	
cover	get done	review	

Some verbs used to describe teaching as establishing a process are:

aid	encourage	free	motivate
arouse	excite	initiate	set up
arrange	expedite	inspire	stimulate
assist	facilitate	liberate	stir

Refer to the notes that you kept for Strategy 2-1, titled "Past Meanings of Teaching." In each of your definitions of what "to teach" means, underline the verbs referring to your actions as a teacher.

Compare your verbs from Strategy 2-1 to the three preceding lists. Which list has verbs that are most similar to yours?

Complete this conclusion sentence:

I understand and experience teaching in terms of

_____.

For the Group

Read your conclusion sentence to your group. Explain the evidence you have for your conclusion.

Strategy 4-2
A Search for an
Occupational
Metaphor

This strategy can help you to identify an occupational metaphor that you may be using to guide your teaching.

For You

Complete this sentence by filling in the information requested in parentheses:

If teaching had not been a possible choice of career, I might have chosen to be a(n) *(name of occupation)*

_____ .

Complete this sentence by filling in the information requested in parentheses:

I understand and experience teaching as if I were a(n) *(name of occupation in preceding blank)*

_____ .

Think about the preceding sentence. To what extent is it true?

For the Group

Explain to the group the ways that you see teaching in terms of your other possible occupation. Also identify ways that teaching seems to differ from that occupation.

Strategy 4-3
A Metaphor
Influenced by a
Significant
Teacher

Use this strategy to identify a metaphor that you may be using to define yourself as a teacher. *Note: To use this strategy effectively, you must first complete Strategy 2-4.*

For You

Complete the following sentences, supplying the information requested in parentheses:

In the RepGrid in Strategy 2-4 ("Significant Teachers"), the teacher most

similar to me was _____ .

In many ways, *(teacher named above)* _____ was

like a *(name of job, role, or relationship)* _____ to me.

Now complete this sentence by filling in the information requested in parentheses:

I understand and experience teaching in terms of *(name of job, role, or relationship just described)*

_____ .

Think about the preceding sentence. To what extent is it true?

For the Group   *Explain to your* group the similarities and differences between the occupation identified in Strategy 4-2 and teaching as it has been perceived in this strategy.

Strategy 4-4   With this strategy, you may find a new way to see yourself as a teacher. *Note:*
A Significant   *To use this strategy effectively, you must first complete Strategy 2-9.*
Other's
Metaphor

For You   *Complete the following* sentence, supplying the information requested in parentheses:

In the Figure 2-7 RepGrid, done in Strategy 2-9 ("Significant Others"), the person who was most intellectually similar to me was *(name of person)*

_____ .

Now complete this sentence by filling in the information requested in parentheses:

I understand and experience teaching in much the same way as a *(occupation of the person just named)*

_____ .

Think about the preceding sentence. To what extent is it true?

For the Group   *Explain to your* group the similarities and differences between the occupation of the significant person that you named and the way that you see teaching. If the person named was a teacher, describe how he or she taught. In what ways do you teach in the same way?

Strategy 4-5
METAPHORS
FROM YOUR
AUTOBIOGRAPHY

This strategy proposes that you search your autobiography for metaphors. *Note: To use this strategy effectively, you must first complete Strategy 2-10.*

For You   *Reread the autobiography* that you wrote for Strategy 2-10 ("Writing Your Autobiography"). Look for places where you experience or explain one thing in terms of another. Compile a list of metaphors in your autobiography.

Select three of these metaphors related to the way you experience education to complete these sentences:

I see_____ as _____.

I understand _____ as _____.

I experience _____ as _____.

For the Group   *Read these sentences* to your group. Ask the members if any of these sentences surprise them.

Strategy 4-6
JOURNAL
METAPHORS

The purpose of this strategy is to reveal the metaphors that you have been using in your journal. *Note: To use this strategy effectively, you must first complete Strategy 3-1.*

For You   *As you reread* your journal, keep the following sentence stems in mind. Complete as many of the sentences as you can.

• I experience *teaching* as if it were _____

_____.

• I experience *students* as if they were _____

_____.

- I experience my *best students* as if they were _____

  _____.

- I experience my most *difficult students* as if they were _____

  _____.

- I experience my *supervisor* as if he/she were _____

  _____.

- I experience my *classroom* as if it were _____

  _____.

- I experience *learning* as if it were _____

  _____.

- I experience the *subjects I teach* as if they were _____

  _____.

- I experience the *school building* as if it were _____

  _____.

- I experience the *central administration* as if it were _____

  _____.

For the Group   Describe to the group any metaphors you found that are particularly clear to you.

Strategy 4-7   This strategy will help you to identify an occupational metaphor central to
SWITCH YOUR   the way you see teaching.
TRAINING

For You   *Complete this sentence:*

Other than education, the training or experience that would have best prepared me for the teaching responsibilities I now have would have been

_____

_____.

Think about the preceding sentence. What does it tell you about how you experience teaching?

For the Group   *On a slip* of paper, write the type of training you identified above and give the paper to one member of your group. That member will read off the types of training written by all group members. Record them below. Predict who would choose each type of training. Reveal your choices and discuss their meaning.

Training	*I believe this type of training was selected by:*
_____	_____
_____	_____
_____	_____
_____	_____
_____	_____
_____	_____
_____	_____

Strategy 4-8
REPGRIDDING
OCCUPATIONS   By using the RepGrid to compare teaching to other occupations, you can gain some insight into the metaphors that you use for teaching.

For You   *Figure 4.1 lists* eight occupations. Note the checkmarks in the first row under *Physician* and *Social Worker*. Are you, as a teacher, more like a physician or social worker? Circle the checkmark under that occupation (if you believe that your teaching is equally similar to both occupations, circle both checkmarks).

• In a word or short phrase, describe how the marked occupation is similar to your teaching. Write the word or phrase in the right-hand column of the figure under the words *Similar to me as a teacher*.

• Note the two checkmarks in the second row under *Parent* and *Politician*. Which of these two occupations is most like your teaching? Circle that checkmark, and describe the similarity in the right-hand column. Continue to compare your teaching with the occupations identified in the remaining 18 rows. Circle the checkmarks and describe the similarities.

The words written on the right are some of your constructs about teaching. They are among the constructs that you use to create metaphors of yourself as a teacher.

Count the checkmarks that you have circled in each column and write those numbers at the bottom of the columns. The occupations with the highest numbers are those you see as the most similar to your teaching. With this information, complete these sentences:

I see myself as a *(specify an occupation)* _____

when _____.

I see myself as a *(specify an occupation)* _____

when _____.

I see myself as a *(specify an occupation)* _____

when _____.

For the Group   Read these sentences to your group. Discuss the similarities and differences in the occupational metaphors you each use to describe your teaching.

Physician	Parent	Social worker	Politician	Actor	Clergy	Laborer	Engineer	Similar to me as a teacher
✔		✔						
	✔		✔					
				✔		✔		
					✔		✔	
✔			✔					
	✔			✔				
		✔			✔			
			✔			✔		
				✔			✔	
			✔		✔			
✔				✔				
	✔				✔			
		✔				✔		
			✔				✔	
✔					✔			
	✔					✔		
		✔					✔	
✔						✔		
	✔						✔	
		✔		✔				
								TOTALS

Strategy 4-9
REPGRIDDING
ADDITIONAL
OCCUPATIONS

By extending Strategy 4-8 using occupations that you select, you can refine your understanding of the occupational metaphors that you use. *Note: To use this strategy effectively, you must first complete Strategy 4-8.*

For You

Along the top of Figure 4.2, list up to eight occupations different from those used in Figure 4.1. Include occupations that you use to describe your teaching. Occupations described by the right-hand column words in the previous strategy are good candidates. Complete the figure according to the same directions as in Strategy 4-8.

Complete this sentence:

At the beginning of a *(specify a period of time)* _____, I often

act as if I were a *(specify an occupation)* _____.

As the *(specify the same period of time)* _____ progresses, I act

more like a *(specify another occupation)* _____.

Select a subject area, class period, or grade level, and complete this sentence:

When I am teaching *(subject, period, or grade)* _____,

I often see myself as a *(specify an occupation)* _____,

but I am more like a *(specify another occupation)* _____

when I am teaching *(subject, period, or grade)* _____.

For the Group

Read to the group the names of the eight occupations that you selected for Figure 4.2. Ask the group: "Of the eight occupations, which do you think that I find my teaching is most similar to most of the time?"

FIGURE 4.2: A RepGrid of Additional Occupations

Similar to me as a teacher

✔		✔						
	✔		✔					
				✔		✔		
					✔		✔	
✔			✔					
	✔		✔					
		✔			✔			
			✔			✔		
				✔			✔	
			✔		✔			
✔				✔				
	✔				✔			
		✔				✔		
			✔				✔	
✔					✔			
	✔					✔		
		✔					✔	
✔						✔		
	✔						✔	
		✔		✔				
								TOTALS

Strategy 4-10
LEARNING FROM YOUR RITUALS

This strategy is designed to help you become more aware of some of your habitual actions and to learn what those actions reveal about how you view teaching.

By identifying your classroom rituals, you can learn about the metaphors you use, for as Lakoff and Johnson (1980) assert, "The values that we live by are perhaps most strongly reflected in the little things we do over and over." That we do them repeatedly does not mean we are aware of what we are doing. In fact, the nature of habitual actions is such that they are likely to be hidden from us. Your students may be more aware of your rituals than you are.

For You   *Ask your students* to respond to these statements:

Some things that *(your name)* _____ says over and over are

(words, phrases, or sentences) _____

_____

_____ .

Some things that *(your name)* _____ does over and over

are *(words, phrases, or sentences)* _____

_____

_____ .

Compile the results of this survey. Choose several statements or actions that are particularly interesting to you.

For the Group   *Reveal the words* and actions to your group. Ask if anyone would be willing to complete this sentence for you:

A teacher who repeatedly *(one of your rituals)* _____

likely sees *(teaching, students, school, or learning)* _____

as *(analog)* _____ .

Strategy 4-11
TAKE IT LITERALLY

By using this strategy, you can evaluate how some of your metaphors influence your effectiveness as a teacher.

For You

To learn about the effectiveness of some of your metaphors, examine the implications of the metaphor in its literal sense. For example, suppose one of the metaphors you hold is *teacher as gardener.* If you were a gardener instead of a teacher, how would your garden look? What plants would it contain? How would you care for the garden? What would be some of your daily tasks?

Now compare this literal picture of you in a garden with you in your classroom. Which of your goals as a gardener are positive as goals for a teacher? Which are of questionable value? Which of your tasks as a gardener are beneficial for your students when you perform those tasks as a teacher? Which might be harmful? What are some strengths in metaphorically viewing yourself as a gardener? What implications would this metaphor have for your teaching?

Complete the following sentence:

One of the metaphors I use to describe myself as a teacher is

_____.

Now visualize yourself as literally being this metaphor, and complete the following sentences:

• Some immediate needs that I would have include:

_____

_____

_____

• Some long-range needs would include:

_____

_____

_____

- Some actions that I would take to meet these needs are:

_____

_____

_____

- Those actions that would benefit my students were I to perform them as a teacher are:

_____

_____

_____

- Those that might be harmful include:

_____

_____

_____

- Some strengths of _____ as a metaphor for me as a

teacher are _____

_____.

- Some weaknesses of _____ as a metaphor for

me as a teacher are_____

_____.

For the Group *Explain to the* group the opinions that you formed about the effectiveness of the metaphor you chose. Ask if anyone sees this metaphor in a different light.

Strategy 4-12
REVERSE THE METAPHOR

This strategy calls for the reversal of some of your teaching metaphors and consideration of the implications of that new metaphor on your students.

For example, you might recognize that one of your metaphors is *teacher as police officer*. How would your classroom be different if the metaphor were reversed to *police officer as teacher?* If an experienced, professional police officer were to replace you as teacher, what strengths would this person bring to your classroom? What difficulties would he or she cause? What does that say about your effectiveness when you experience teaching in terms of police work?

For You   *Complete these sentences* by filling in the information requested in parentheses or necessary after colons:

- A metaphor that I use to describe myself as a teacher is *(occupation)*

_____.

- Imagine that an experienced, professional *(same occupation)* _____ were teaching in your classroom. This person would be effective in these ways:

_____

_____

_____

Some problems this person would have teaching my students are:

_____

_____

_____

For the Group   *Complete this sentence:*

My students benefit when I act as a _____ because

_____

_____.

Ask if someone in the group will complete this sentence about you:

When you act as a _____, your students

may have some difficulty because_____

_____.

Strategy 4-13
MIXED METAPHORS

This strategy helps you to identify compatible and conflicting metaphors that you use for yourself, your students, and your classroom.

The reason that this effort is important is that your metaphors for the various aspects of your work are not always compatible. If, for example, you picture the *teacher as guide* and the *students as slugs*, you are likely to be frequently frustrated. Your life would likely be smoother if you changed the first metaphor to *teacher as lettuce* or changed the second to *students as curious tourists*.

In his research on teachers' metaphors, Gregory Marchant (1991) has had teachers select metaphors from lists. Adaptations of three of Marchant's lists follow.

For You

Circle as many as six metaphors on this list that describe the way you see yourself as a teacher.

actor	doctor	master	prison warden
advocate	encyclopedia	mastermind	projectionist
animal trainer	enemy	minister	referee
artist	entrepreneur	movie director	shepherd
audience	farmer	neighbor	slave
boss	fountain	orchestra conductor	soldier
brother or sister	friend	parent	student
coach	guide	party host	victim
comedian	host	police officer	
counselor	judge	politician	

other _____

From the next list of metaphors, circle up to six that describe the way you see your students.

actor	daughter or son	monster	questioner
advisee	employee	musician	sheep
athlete	enemy	neighbor	slave
audience	farm animal	obstacle	sponge
ball of clay	farm crop	offender	teacher
brother or sister	friend	parishioner	tourist
client	guest	patient	voter
cup	jury	pawn	wild animal
customer	master	prisoner	

other _____

Circle up to six of these metaphors to describe your classroom.

animal den	courtroom	home	prison
battlefield	factory	hospital	resort
cage	family	jungle	small business
carnival	farm	library	stage
church	fishbowl	meadow	test
circus	foreign land	movie	treatment room
community	gameboard	party	zoo
concert	gym	playground	

other _____

List the metaphors that you selected:

Teacher metaphors	*Student metaphors*	*Classroom metaphors*
1. _____	1. _____	1. _____
2. _____	2. _____	2. _____
3. _____	3. _____	3. _____
4. _____	4. _____	4. _____
5. _____	5. _____	5. _____
6. _____	6. _____	6. _____

Which of these metaphors describe contrasting and conflicting images? Which metaphors are compatible, fitting together as a set to comprise a single larger metaphor? With this information, complete this sentence:

At times, I see my classroom as a _____

with me as_____

and my students as _____.

For the Group   *Describe to your* group the conflicting and compatible metaphors that you found. Ask if anyone can suggest how changing some of the metaphors could eliminate the conflicts.

Strategy 4-14   This strategy describes a technique for evaluating the potential usefulness of
MATCHED   new classroom materials by matching their metaphors with yours. If you are
METAPHORS   aware of the metaphors used in instructional materials, you can make more
informed decisions about how useful the materials would be to you. *Note: To use this strategy effectively, you must first complete Strategy 4-13.*

Seldom do you adopt new curriculum materials or classroom management approaches entirely as the developers intended. A primary reason for this need to customize is that developers have one set of metaphors for learning, instruction, content, teachers, students, and motivation, while you have another set. Thus, you adapt new materials to fit your beliefs. The parts of the materials that you use will be ones that match your metaphors or can be adapted to do so.

The task of identifying metaphors is not simple. Materials developers are not likely to list the metaphors that they are using. You will need to infer those metaphors from the words being used and from the nature of the activities themselves.

For You   *Figure 4.3 lists* the metaphors used by two approaches to cooperative learning and by hands-on science. Note how the six metaphors within each approach are in harmony with each other. Using data gathered in previous strategies, particularly Strategy 4-13, write a set of your teaching metaphors in the "My metaphors" column in Figure 4.3. Determine whether your metaphors are in harmony with any of the other three sets.

At the top of the right-hand column in Figure 4.3, name some materials that you are considering for classroom use. From your knowledge of these mate-

	Cooperative learning A	Cooperative learning B	Hands-on science	My metaphors	Other material
Learning	memorizing landmarks	solving challenges	abstracting from the concrete	_____	_____
Teaching	mapping out new territory	setting up "dangerous" situations	providing solvable puzzles	_____	_____
Content	landmarks	survival skills	products of science	_____	_____
Teacher	guide	controller	mirror	_____	_____
Student	one of a pack of explorers	person in need of help	tinkerer	_____	_____
Motivation	approval of fellow explorers	survival	curiosity	_____	_____

rials, identify the metaphors used in each of the six areas listed in the left-hand column.

For the Group   *Describe the match* between the metaphors used by the materials you selected and your own metaphors. Evaluate the usefulness of these materials for you.

Strategy 4-15
I USED TO BE A
TEACHER WHO...   The purpose of this strategy is for you to reconsider past responses in light of the new insights that you have gained from the strategies in this chapter. *Note: To use this strategy effectively, you must first complete Strategies 2-11 and 3-14.*

For You   *Go back and* review your responses to Strategies 2-11 and 3-14. See if you would change anything now.

For the Group   *Describe to the* group one significant difference in your earlier and current responses.

Strategy 4-16
WHY I AM DOING THIS

The purpose of this strategy is to identify the factors that influence you in making professional choices and to identify new types of choices that you would like to make in the future. This strategy, which also concludes Chapter 3, is here to encourage you to rethink the whos and whys of you as a teacher.

For You

In response to the prompts that follow, describe who you are as a teacher, why you are that way, and what you might do differently. This analysis cannot be extensive. Limit the comments to a few facets of yourself. Also, do not denigrate yourself. Doing so is likely to result in guilt and attempts to excuse, rather than in understanding yourself. Focus on writing positive, nonjudgmental statements.

Who I am as a teacher—

_____

_____

_____

Why I am who I am—

_____

_____

_____

What I might do differently—

_____

_____

_____

For the Group

In telling your group "Who I am," "Why I am," and "What I might do differently," limit yourself to relating only those insights that you have experienced since you began meeting with your group (if you completed Strategy 3-14, you may each describe some significant difference in your responses since that time). Further restrict your comments to positive, uncritical statements about yourself.

References   Lakoff, George, and Mark Johnson. 1980. *Metaphors We Live By*. Chicago: University of Chicago Press.

Marchant, Gregory. "Examining Metaphors in Teaching Through the Use of Simile Lists." Paper presented at the annual meeting of the American Educational Research Association, Chicago, April 1991.

Tobin, Kenneth. 1990. "Changing Metaphors and Beliefs: A Master Switch for Teaching?" *Theory into Practice* 29(2): 122–127.

CHAPTER 5

HEARING YOUR STUDENTS

Like you, your students are not passive recipients. They interact with the world to try to make sense of it. They each build a model of life in general, of the subjects that you teach, of your classroom, of you. How they see each of these elements determines how they respond to it. For example, how they see you determines, in part, their behavior toward you.

Your students do not see you in the same way that you see yourself. How you really are has no meaning for them. What they act on is their perceptions of you. Furthermore, since everyone has a unique perspective, everyone's perceptions can be thought of as correct.

Take your students' constructs seriously, for telling students that they are wrong in the way that they perceive the world devalues their experience and leads to confusion and alienation. Try instead to see your students as just as constantly involved as you are in hypothesizing and testing.

It is important to remember, too, that this forming and testing of hypotheses does not always involve activity. In fact, passivity is itself often a way of testing hypotheses.

The strategies in this chapter are designed to make you more aware of the ways that your students perceive the world. This information can help you understand their behavior better and lead to better choices by both you and your students.

While the strategies ask you to gather responses from groups of students, be careful not to combine these findings into "the student point of view." Their constructs are as complex as your own and probably more contradictory. In your reading of responses and in your group discussions, be more alert for the significant and the unique than for commonalities.

Naturally, if it were possible to characterize students with a single description, teaching would be simpler. The information you get from these strategies, however, will not simplify your task. Indeed it is likely to make it more complicated—but also more successful.

As you proceed, acknowledge (to yourself at least) the uneven power relationship that you have with students. Because of it, some of your students will respond to your questions by asking themselves, "How does this teacher want me to answer?" Keep this accommodating tendency in mind when you select and organize the strategies. Ask yourself, "How can I diminish this power differential in order to get honest responses?"

Verbal promises of confidentiality and assurances that "This is for your benefit…" will not prevent students from telling you what they think you want to hear. As alternatives, consider small, student-led groups, private out-of-class discussions, and other such means of de-emphasizing your teacher role.

Along the way, tell your students why you want to know what they believe. Explain your ideas on how you can learn what they think. Allow them to suggest better ways of doing it. Above all, never use student responses in an attempt to control their behavior or beliefs.

These strategies are written in the language of the middle and secondary school student, but they are useful for students at all levels. The strategies can easily be adapted for younger students and still keep their intent.

Many of the strategies in Chapters 2, 3, and 4, which you used to learn about your own beliefs, can be adapted so that students can learn more about themselves. Consider using some of those strategies as you select techniques for your students.

To make efficient use of time, however, consider having some members of the group use one strategy while others use a different one. This approach forestalls the need for everyone in your group to carry out all the strategies with all of his or her students. Discuss your experiences and decide which strategies would be valuable for all of you to use on a wider scale.

Strategy 5-1
STUDENT CONSTRUCTS

You can use this strategy to learn what your students perceive as your constructs of a successful student. The strategy was developed by C. T. P. Diamond (1991), who in turn used Kelly's (1955) personal construct theory.

For You

Say to your students: "A friend of yours is planning to take this class next year. He or she has asked you what he or she must do to succeed in this class. Explain what your friend must do to get the highest possible grade."

Record particularly revealing excerpts:

_____

_____

_____

_____

_____

_____

For the Group   *Compare your students'* responses with those of the rest of your group. Together, select what you consider to be significant viewpoints. Why do you think that some students perceive your classes in these ways? What are the implications of these perceptions for your teaching?

Strategy 5-2
SCHOOL GROUPS   With this strategy, you can get information about school social groups and how they are viewed by insiders and outsiders of those groups.

Some students use a great deal of energy in seeking and maintaining membership in school groups. The identities they seek for themselves and assign to others are a source of powerful constructs about school.

For You   *Ask your students* to name some of the informal social groupings present in your school. Without comment, write these names on the chalkboard. Then ask each student to:

- Write the name of the group that you believe you are in.
- Explain what another student would have to have or do to get into your group.
- Name the alternate group that you would choose if you could not be in the group that you are in now.
- Explain what you would have to have or do to get into that group.

Compile the results for each group in the following format:

*(group name)*_____

As seen by themselves   *As seen by others*

_____   _____

_____   _____

_____   _____

• •

_____   _____

_____   _____

_____   _____

*(group name)*_____

As seen by themselves   *As seen by others*

_____   _____

_____   _____

_____   _____

_____   _____

_____   _____

For the Group   *Determine which social* groups do well in school. Which do poorly? Discuss what might be done to give the low-achieving groups a greater chance of school success.

Strategy 5-3
GETTING SOME
CULTURE   This strategy provides a means by which you can observe some of your students' cultural experiences.

For You   *Ask your students* to write responses to these questions about their plans for the upcoming weekend:

- If you were to see a movie, what would it likely be?
- What TV shows are you likely to watch?
- What are you likely to read?
- What music will you listen to?

Try to identify at least two patterns in the students' responses. What you are looking for is not simply minor variations in entertainment preferences, but significantly different tastes that typify different cultures.

	Pattern A	*Pattern B*
Movies	_____	_____
TV	_____	_____
Reading	_____	_____
Music	_____	_____

For the Group   *With the group,* identify at least two differing student cultures. Plan how you, alone or with group members, could immerse yourself in at least one of those cultures for at least half a day. Then discuss the implications of your experiences on your teaching.

Strategy 5-4
IMPORTANT
KNOWLEDGE

This strategy is designed to reveal the types of knowledge that your students consider important.

For You   *Ask your students* this question: "Considering your life both in and out of school, what is the most important lesson you have learned in the past year?" Analyze the responses and answer the following questions.

• What are some of the most significant lessons that students learned?

_____

_____

_____

• Where are some places that this learning occurred?

_____

_____

_____

• What important people facilitated this learning?

_____

_____

_____

For the Group *Discuss the implications* of your findings on what is taught in your classes and your school.

Strategy 5-5
IMPORTANT
ASPECTS OF
SUBJECTS

Use this strategy to find out what your students believe is important about the subjects that you teach.

Students are not often asked about what they value in a class, possibly because teachers view the students' perspective as too narrow to validly determine what should be taught. While that may be true, student values are very important because they unquestionably influence what students learn.

For You *Have students complete* the statements that follow. The issue of whether students are to consider only course content should intentionally be left open to invite broader responses.

• The one thing about this class that:
1. is most important to know is—
2. is most interesting is—
3. is most useful is—
4. I wish we would learn about is—
5. will certainly not be discussed is—
6. is not at all important is—

Identify some unique answers that seem to carry universal meaning.

For the Group *Identify one implication* of the information gathered that you all absolutely will not accept.

References Diamond, C. T. P. 1991. *Teacher Education As Transformation.* Philadelphia: Open University Press.

Kelly, George. 1955. *Psychology of Personal Constructs.* London: Norton.

CHAPTER 6

THREE APPROACHES TO RESEARCH

If you have been a member of a group using the strategies described in previous chapters, you have probably already changed some of your teaching behaviors. Why? Because when you examine what you believe and what you do, it is almost inevitable that you will find areas that you want to change.

This chapter and the next two offer guidance in how you can more formally initiate and evaluate change in your teaching practice. The process recommended is known as teacher-based action research (T-BAR). T-BAR is a tool with the potential to help you improve what you do, even as you gain a more acute understanding of what it is that you do.

Actually, you have already begun to use T-BAR. By critically examining what you do as a teacher, you have taken the first step in the process. The next steps of T-BAR involve selection of a topic for study, development of a plan of action, implementation of the plan, collection of evaluative data, interpretation of the information collected, and revision of the initial plan.

While this sequence might sound like the problem-solving method commonly used by traditional educational researchers and by classroom teachers seeking solutions to everyday problems, T-BAR is, in practice, quite different. Figure 6.1 summarizes the differences in the three approaches for solving educational problems.

By comparing T-BAR to two problem-solving approaches that you already know about, you can get a clearer picture of how you can use T-BAR. Thus, the remainder of this chapter describes each of the three techniques in more detail.

An Example of Traditional Educational Research

Douglass Maunder, a professor of educational psychology at a local university, is extremely knowledgeable about interpersonal needs theory. He speculates that students who have a high need to be included will try to fill this need by making contact with their peers during breaks between school class periods. To test this notion, he decides to investigate this hypothesis:

FIGURE 6.1: DIFFERENCES IN THREE TYPES OF EDUCATIONAL RESEARCH

Traditional Educational Research	Classroom Teacher Research	Teacher-Based Action Research (T-BAR)
The problem arises from:		
an implication of an interpretation of a theory	a blockage to a goal	a desire to improve practice
The purpose of the research is to:		
support a hypothesis that applies across populations	solve an immediate problem	construct knowledge about self and situations and to take practice in new directions
The proposed action is based on:		
reflection upon theory	initial perceptions	reflection upon perceptions
The focus of the research is on:		
theory	practice	practice/theory as a single concept
Colleagues are used as:		
a source of theory and as critics of work	a source of possible solutions	mutual reflectors
The relationship of the investigator to the student is as:		
observer to subject	problem solver to problem source	learner to learner
Successful research brings about change in:		
universal understandings	technique	values and understandings of self and situations

*A positive relationship exists between middle school students'
inclusion needs scores as measured on the FIRO-B (Fundamental
Interpersonal Relations Orientation-Behavior instrument) and the
number of peers to whom they speak during class breaks.*

In a large nearby school district, Maunder has established a mutually
respectful relationship with the central office administrator who approves all
research projects in the district. Maunder submits a formal proposal that
explains the purpose of the project and requests the participation of two
middle schools.

After approval, Maunder and the district administrator meet with principals
of targeted schools to seek their involvement in the project. The proposal
stipulates the use of wall-mounted video cameras to "study student interaction during class breaks." Maunder and the administrator assure the principals that no judgments will be made about the schools, that only Maunder
and his graduate assistants will view the tapes, and that neither the schools
nor the district would be identified in any research reports. The principals
agree to let their schools participate in the study.

Each principal informs the students and teachers in the school that a study
will be done and that it will involve the videotaping of class breaks. Everyone
is assured that no one in the school district will view the tapes to check on
student behavior. Students and teachers are told to just ignore the cameras
and act naturally.

Two graduate students who do not know the students or their FIRO-B
scores view the tapes and code behaviors. The next year, Maunder reads his
paper reporting the findings of the study at a national convention.
Afterward, he sends a copy of the paper to the central office administrator,
along with thanks for her cooperation. The administrator files the report.

Traditional Educational Research Described

Traditional educational research, Maunder's specialty, is essentially the posi-
tivist model of the natural sciences imported into the social sciences. This
model is behaviorist, that is, events are thought to occur as a result of prior
causal actions. This way of thinking leads to research findings that are
expressed as cause and effect statements, such as:

- As teachers increase the wait time after asking questions, critical thinking
  increases.

- If teachers do not reward students for inappropriate behaviors, the rate at
  which these behaviors occur diminishes.

- If a lesson contains an advance organizer, more students accomplish learning objectives.

How traditional researchers formulate such testable ideas, or hypotheses, is a relatively obscure step in the scientific method—the source of hypotheses is often seen as an almost mystical element in an otherwise rational enterprise. Often, if a researcher is reflecting on a theory, saying something like "If this theory is true, then one would expect... ," a novel implication just seems to pop into the researcher's mind. However they derive hypotheses, though, productive researchers are certain to be people with a solid understanding of their respective fields.

Although Maunder's hypothesis had logical connections to theory, the supposition had to be tested to see if it was supported in the observable world. If so, the hypothesis might ultimately be established as a generalizable principle of teaching or learning.

To test the hypothesis, a representative sample of the universe is selected for investigation. Objective observers then use techniques and instruments designed to give unbiased measures of preselected variables. Although this representational testing is carried out locally, the results will be advanced as universally applicable.

The subjects of Maunder's investigation did not know the real purpose of the study. Had they known, that, in itself, might have influenced behavior and thereby invalidated the experiment. Objectivity is vital to traditional educational research.

Maunder's fellow researchers serve two primary functions. First, they are the source of theoretical foundations from which the hypothesis emerged. Second, once the study is completed, they judge its validity.

Traditional educational research is regarded as successful if it changes the research community's understanding of how teaching or learning occurs. The value of a study is not decided by how much it changes professional practice in the classroom. Although the research does have an important effect on practice, the primary goal of traditional educational research is the development and refinement of theory.

The model in Figure 6.2 summarizes the characteristics of one type of traditional educational research. On the basis of an understanding of theory, the researcher poses a possible relationship, or hypothesis. A plan of action is undertaken to test the hypothesis. As the plan is carried out, detached observers make objective measurements. If interpretation of the resulting data support the hypothesis, new relationships may be established and the theory is strengthened.

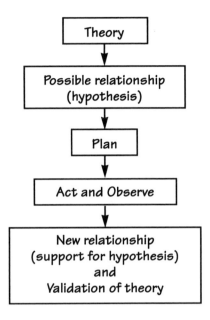

An Example of Classroom Teacher Research

At the beginning of the school year, the students in Steve Vivum's seventh grade life science classes came into the classroom quickly and promptly. By February, though, they seemed to drag into class. Many students would stand in the hallway until the bell rang and then straggle into the classroom. Some students would often be a minute or so late. This pattern is a rerun of last year, Vivum's first, but now the problem seems more pronounced.

Since Vivum likes to chat with students at the beginning of each period, he knew that the tardy students were not missing any science content. However, Catherine Alstern, Vivum's team leader, spoke to him about the problem of students congregating outside the classroom and blocking traffic.

Vivum talked with several other teachers about how they get their students into the room. He received many suggestions. All of them had to do with setting clear expectations and administering swift penalties for noncompliance. Suggested reprimands ranged from administrative referral and parental contact, on through the lowering of grades, all the way to public humiliation.

Alstern suggested a slightly different method. Vivum should stand outside his door during breaks and ask students to move into the room. Then just before the bell, Vivum should move to the front of the class. Right after the bell, the lesson should begin.

Vivum tried Alstern's ideas. They solved the problem of the students blocking the hallway, but some students continued to arrive late, and Vivum missed talking with his students.

Classroom Teacher Research Described

Classroom teachers become motivated to change when they are prevented from reaching a goal. For example, students' poor study habits, obstreperous classroom behavior, or slow learning rates may block a teacher's goal of having students like the class, show active involvement, achieve high test scores, behave in an orderly manner, or make the teacher look good to a supervisor. In Vivum's case, students' reluctance to enter his classroom blocked his goal of appearing competent to his team leader.

As Vivum looked for a way to change his practice, his judgments about the nature of the problem came from what he saw happening. He identified the problem as lingering students. He did not consider that the dawdling might be a symptom of another problem.

Vivum next matched his perception of the problem against possible solutions. He first went to his memory to find a solution that had worked for him in similar situations in the past. Not confident with what he found there, he searched his memory further for some ideas from his readings and his coursework. He then sought the advice of some trusted colleagues.

The possible solution that Vivum chose was in some ways like an educational researcher's hypothesis. First, it was an idea that needed testing, and second, the validity of the hypothesis depended upon what happened when the idea was applied in the real world.

Note, however, two significant differences in the educational researcher's and the teacher-researcher's hypotheses. One is the reason that the hypothesis was created. The educational researcher was looking for insights into the teaching and learning process, while the teacher-researcher was trying to remove something blocking him from a goal. The other difference lies in the basis of each hypothesis. The educational researcher's hypothesis was rooted in knowledge of and reflection on theory. The teacher-researcher's possible solution was based on his perception of what was blocking his goal.

Moreover, the relationship of each investigator to the students was different. To the educational researcher, the student was a subject whose behavior was observed to furnish evidence that either strengthened or weakened the hypothesis as a universal truth. To the teacher-researcher, the student was considered to be the source of a problem. The teacher-researcher's task was to find a solution, a teaching technique that was new to the problematic situation.

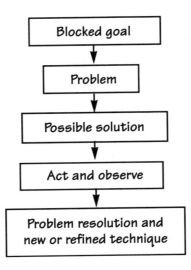

Figure 6.3 illustrates the aspects of classroom teacher problem solving. The problem arises when a goal is blocked. The experiences of the teacher and other practitioners suggest a plan of action to solve the problem. The plan is carried out, and its effectiveness in removing the block is observed. If the intervention is effective, the problem is resolved, and a new or refined technique is added to the teacher's repertoire.

An Example of Teacher-Based Action Research

Terri Barr met weekly with five middle school teacher colleagues to examine teaching beliefs and practices. In the fifth month of this process, the group became aware of a common concern. Experience had led them to anticipate that, as the school year progressed, the incidence of inappropriate student behavior was likely to increase. The teachers knew that, if this previously noted pattern were to recur, they were likely to change their teaching behaviors and attitudes toward students in ways that they would not like.

To stimulate reflection on these concerns, Barr's group devoted its next three meetings to consideration of a series of questions:

- What, exactly, are the problematic behaviors that are likely to increase in frequency?

- Are any positive behaviors likely to increase at the same time?

- What do these behaviors indicate about students' needs?

- Will teacher behaviors also reflect a lack of enthusiasm for school work?

- Is the lack of enthusiasm among students and teachers limited to school work?

- Is enthusiasm greater in some areas of life than others? Some areas of school than others? If so, what characterizes these areas?

- Are some students and some teachers more enthusiastic than others? If so, what characterizes them?

The members of the group discussed these questions among themselves, with other teachers, and with students. Some useful ideas emerged from this process. The teachers realized that enthusiasm is rekindled when new possibilities are opened, when personal interests are met, when connections are made between and among different aspects of life, and when people work with others to accomplish common goals.

As a result of reflection on their series of questions, the group agreed that the goal of their research would be:

> *To increase student and teacher interest in school learning activities during the second half of the year.*

In an effort to deepen their understanding and to pique students' and teachers' interest, each of the six teachers next identified new actions to take.

Barr and Victoria Anglaise, who, respectively, are social studies and English teachers on the same eighth grade team, decided to jointly plan a two-week project comparing and contrasting two neighborhood restaurants—a fast-food chain restaurant and a locally owned, sit-down establishment. Groups would compare and contrast aspects of the restaurants such as history, environmental impact, future, and how each meets the needs of the customers, employees, supervisor, and owner. Barr was to work with four-student teams on the research design. Anglaise would work with the same students on writing research reports. The unit also featured a fact-finding field trip to each restaurant.

The earth science teacher, Tara Firma, planned to work with her students to select the subject area for their next unit of study. The science classes formulated the questions to be answered and developed ways to find the answers.

Art Painter asked each art student to create a work related to something being studied in another class. The students eventually presented their works to the selected classes, requested written responses from students and teachers, and on the basis of that feedback, assigned themselves grades for the projects.

Teachers Michael Gourmand (home economics) and Connie Maps (social studies) collaboratively planned a unit on Guatemala. For a week in Gourmand's class, the students would prepare Guatemalan dishes, in addition to exploring the locale's native foods, eating customs, and preparation methods. The next week, in Maps's classes, the students studied the effects of history, geography, economics, and religion on the foods of the Guatemalans.

Before beginning their projects, these teachers tried to predict how each investigation might increase student and teacher interest and how the new lessons might help everyone understand student and teacher motivation. The group developed several ways to collect data, and while carrying out each study, they met twice to discuss preliminary results. Upon completion of the units, each teacher or pair of teachers presented a brief formal summary of their findings.

With the new knowledge, the same group of teachers designed and carried out a second cycle of new approaches to the initial goal. After the second cycle, they formulated a different and more specific goal:

To develop teaching approaches designed to meet students' interests.

A third cycle focused on this more circumscribed goal.

Ultimately, the entire group collaborated on the writing of a 40-page research report titled "Relating Instruction to the Interests of Middle School Students." Barr, Maps, and Painter gave a presentation on this subject at a state teachers' conference.

Teacher-Based Action Research Described

Barr and her colleagues initiated teacher-based action research to improve the quality of their teaching. They believed that they would benefit doubly from their research, because they would not only be taking their teaching practice in new directions, but they would also be gaining new knowledge about themselves, their students, and the situations in which they taught. They could realistically feel confident of success because of their collective experience, the insights that they gained from group discussions, and the invigorating sense of collegiality in the group.

While the group members' action plans were rooted in how each member perceived and anticipated student and teacher behaviors, the perceptions selected as important were greatly influenced by several months of reflection, and that reflection took place *before* any specific actions were planned. Furthermore, although the group members served each other in multiple ways, using each other as critics of work done and as a source of ideas for

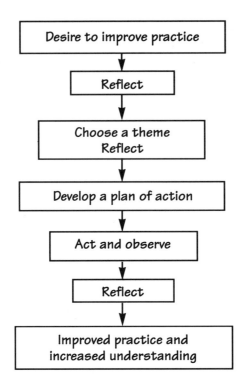

new directions, their most valuable contribution to each other was in the high level of reflection that is possible in this type of group.

The Barr group's focus was on changing practice, but it accomplished much more than that. The teachers did change practice by developing and implementing new instructional approaches and materials, but they also came away with new understanding (read theories) of what makes lessons work.

To label understanding as *theory* and somehow separate it from *practice* is to create an unproductive division. The T-BAR group did not do that. Instead, they created for themselves new *theory/practice*, or to be visually more accurate, *theorypractice*, or, perhaps, *theoractice*. There is even an established alternative, if you like. It is the existing word, *praxis*, which means informed practice and therefore comes pretty close to describing unified theory and practice.

The relationship between teachers and their students in the T-BAR research was quite distinct from that of the other two research approaches just described. In T-BAR, teachers and students all see themselves as learners. To the teachers, the students were not subjects to be studied or the source of problems to be solved. The students were viewed as a major source of answers to teachers' questions.

Teacher-based action research succeeds when teachers change or confirm values about teaching and learning. It succeeds when teachers' practice takes inventive new directions. It succeeds when teachers develop a deeper understanding of their professional selves, others, and situations.

The stages of teacher-based action research are summarized in Figure 6.4. T-BAR emerges from a teacher's desire to improve practice. Systematic reflection on practice can suggest possible changes in practice that have the potential to yield new insights into practice. Making the changes and carefully observing their effects can provide information for new reflection leading to both deeper understanding and improved practice.

Is T-BAR for You?

Each method of educational research described in this chapter is an effective means of reaching a particular type of goal. Accordingly, in determining the value of any of these methods for you, you must consider how *its* ends match *your* needs.

For instance, if you want to help students who are having difficulty grasping a particular idea, you are likely to find that the problem-solving techniques of classroom teacher research are the best means of reaching your goals. The broadly stated principles of learning derived from traditional educational research will not help you very much in this situation, and T-BAR's ability to help reframe problems and better understand yourself, your situation, and your goals will not bring about the immediate solution required.

If, on the other hand, your interest is in developing a universal understanding of why students drop out of school, traditional research is a likely method of choice. Classroom teacher research methods might help you find a way to help a particular student find a purpose in school, but at best, that would be a small step toward your goal. Using T-BAR to explore your school and your goals in order to see your situation in new ways would also fail to yield a broad understanding of why students drop out.

But say that you want to look at your daily challenges in new ways. T-BAR can aid you toward that end much more effectively than the two other approaches. Continuing to use existing techniques for getting around blocks to your goals is likely to keep you mired in your old patterns. The methods and broad sweep of traditional research findings are not very applicable to your goal.

In addition to considering the ends that you want, you must also consider how compatible each of these three problem-solving approaches is with your way of thinking. Since teacher problem solving has been the primary technique for finding solutions to classroom problems, its use is not likely to interfere with classroom functioning.

On the other hand, if you are a teacher who wants to maintain tight control of problem identification and solution options, T-BAR's open discussion of problems and possible solutions are likely to conflict with your needs. Some aspects of traditional educational research might also clash with some of your values as a teacher. It may be difficult, for example, for you to be an unbiased observer in your classroom. How fortunate it is that it is unlikely that you even want to be one. Your success as a teacher may well be a function of the investment that you make in your students as people. The very act of divesting yourself of this interest might well diminish your effectiveness in your primary professional role.

A Few Words of Caution

Today's society accords high value to traditional scientific research. Such esteem, in many cases, is well-deserved. If, however, you hold the model of traditional educational research as the only effective path to truth about education, you will necessarily find that teacher-based action research falls short. After all, if one thing is best, anything that differs from it is not as good.

Don't make that comparison. T-BAR and traditional educational research are not competitors. The ends of each type of research are different, and each path can be the best route to its own end. Traditional educational research is an effective way to establish theory. T-BAR is an effective way to improve *your* practice. The validity of T-BAR should be judged on its own merits.

CHAPTER 7

STARTING WITH T-BAR

This chapter suggests ways that you and your T-BAR group can plan and carry out research projects to improve the quality of your teaching. This discussion identifies decisions that you will need to make and describes techniques that can aid you in making these decisions.

A group that uses T-BAR selects a theme—some area of concern—for teacher-based action research projects. Members of the group identify some ways to change their teaching behaviors to address the chosen theme. The effects of these new behaviors are observed and their meanings are discussed. Other desirable changes are identified and carried out. The effects are observed and discussed. Thus the pattern can repeat, on and on toward the constant refinement of teaching.

One possibly misleading aspect of this linear model, however, is that although it accurately describes T-BAR, it does not necessarily describe the path that you will take in your own research. You may start in the middle, jump to another place, move out for a while, and come back in at still another spot. Since it is not possible to predict how your group will work, the process is described as if it were linear.

Why a Group? A teacher working alone can do certain types of action research effectively. And there are, of course, some advantages to solo efforts—you have no need to find others to work with you, to take time to work for consensus about the nature of your research, or to discuss the meaning of your project.

Going through such processes, however, can improve the quality of your research. Communication with the group helps you clarify your thinking. The group serves as a source of ideas. The differing perspectives of group members can give you insights into meaning. In the group, you have informed individuals who can act as observers for you, and you have critical friends to act as an audience for your findings. To capture all these advantages, T-BAR is, ideally, a group process.

A couple of other advantages to working in a group are not so obvious. One is that group work reduces the likelihood that an "anything goes" attitude will seep into your work. Sometimes it is very tempting to justify your classroom practices with a simple "It works for me." Normally, to such a remark, a colleague is likely to respond with "Okay. Whatever works for you." Your group is not likely to be so uncritically accepting. While respecting your individuality and prerogatives, they might ask, "In what sense does it work?" or "How do you know that it works?" While we each need to find our own answers, every answer that we find is not a best one. A group can usually generate more critical reflection and alternatives than someone working alone.

A second subtle advantage of a group is clout. Improving your practice alone, as important as that is, is but one step in improving the total professional environment. By involving other professionals in T-BAR, you multiply the effect of the changes that you make. Even working with just one other person can increase the potential benefit to you and your students.

When you agree to join with others to form a T-BAR group, you are agreeing to a process. You are accepting the belief that working with a group of critical colleagues and friends can help you clarify what you believe, identify discrepancies between your values and your practice, develop new practices that are more in harmony with your beliefs, and evaluate the effects of changes that you make in your teaching. You are not agreeing to agree on how to teach. You are not agreeing to adopt any particular set of values about teaching, schools, or students.

If you catch yourself trying to prove that another group member holds an incorrect value, you are misapplying T-BAR. The aim of T-BAR is not agreement on a correct way to teach. In a T-BAR group, you can ask any member to clarify a belief. You can ask for evidence in support of a belief. Such requests further the ultimate aims of T-BAR, which are helping everyone to critically examine their values about teaching and to investigate improvements in their teaching. This goal is significantly different from establishing *the* way to teach.

Furthermore, if your group members find themselves congratulating each other on how much more correct you are in your approach to teaching than are colleagues who are not in the group, then the group is misreading the intent of T-BAR. Such criticism of others may, in fact, help you to avoid critical self-evaluation. Hold your congratulations for the new insights that you gain into your own practice.

Using the Strategies
The best path for you to take depends on your situation. Your group will need to decide where you are in the T-BAR process and what you need to do to progress.

Look at Strategies 7-1 to 7-6, which will help define the T-BAR process for you. Decide if you want to use the strategies as they are, adapt them, or develop your own agenda. If you have worked through the earlier chapters, you have the necessary skills and experience.

If you are just forming a group and want to begin at this point, read Chapter 1 on group organization and make the necessary beginning decisions. Also consider working through some strategies in Chapters 2 through 7. Doing so now is likely to save time in the future.

Choosing a Theme
Your group needs to select a theme as a focus for its work. One theme that you already have in common is that you are all in T-BAR to move your practice closer to what you believe to be good teaching. Such a theme, however, is probably too general. The more specific you are, the more focused your interaction will be and the more synergistic your individual project effects will be.

Try to identify precisely what you want to improve. Make the theme as specific as you can while maintaining or increasing the eagerness of each member to proceed with his or her research. As a group, talk about how you can develop:

- higher levels of…
- new ways to…
- increased understanding of…

As you work on choosing a theme, make your decisions by consensus. Avoid taking votes. Each of you will have to work hard researching your theme, and if you are outvoted, it is easy to lose enthusiasm.

Also, everyone should remain open to new possibilities. Although it may be unclear to you how a particular theme might affect your work, respect the enthusiasm of your colleagues as an indication of its potential. Remember that all decisions are tentative. Any of them can be changed if you find that they do not prove fruitful. Make your decisions in that spirit.

Work, too, toward clarity. Most themes (some are listed in Figure 7.1) at first sound acceptable. Resist passive acceptance. Question the key words in each proposed theme. Ask what exactly is meant by words like *ethnicity*, *student choice*, *structure of the subject matter*, and *authentic learning activities*.

- Overcome student and/or teacher apathy.
- Improve students' understanding of the structure of the subject matter.
- Increase the number of decisions that students make about their learning activities.
- Broaden the ethnicity of classroom work.
- Establish gender equity in the classroom.
- Change our teaching metaphors.
- Develop new forms of student assessment.
- Strengthen school-community linkages.
- Establish positive school-home connections.
- Make learning activities more authentic.

How does the professional literature define these terms? How does each person in the group define them? No amount of talk can make all these meanings the same, but it can help clarify each other's meanings. Moreover, it is not necessary to agree. You each might have different meanings for a phrase such as *changing my metaphors of teaching*, yet you all can still use that theme for your T-BAR. What is important is that you have a clear understanding of the meaning that you each give the words of the theme.

If you find subgroups emerging with differing levels of enthusiasm for various themes, it may be wise for your group to reorganize into separate groups. Do not move precipitously in this direction, though. Deliberate first, keeping in mind that the primary purpose of getting involved in T-BAR is to improve education, and improving the way people work together is central to that goal. If splitting the group is done because of unresolved conflict or to avoid conflict, the problem is likely to recur in the newly formed groups. Before dismantling the original group, try to identify and resolve whatever divides you.

As you talk about themes, consider keeping all of your community informed about your discussions. You may discover that other people want to research the theme that you have chosen. If so, it might be wise to invite those individuals to join your group.

All efforts to improve education have political aspects, so when you make decisions, keep their political implications in mind. Ask yourselves whether the group work is promoting community or divisiveness. Consider the effects of your actions on the total school milieu. Don't talk yourself into inaction, though. Remember that it is sometimes necessary for part of a community to act before any change will occur on a large scale.

Designing Action Plans Once a theme is selected, each group member will design a plan of action. Develop your plan in response to the question:

Realistically and within the framework of our theme, what can I change that will (1) improve my teaching by making my actual practices more harmonious with what I value as good teaching and (2) help me gain new insights into my teaching?

Your plan should respond to your needs and the needs of your students, but down the line you may want to consider the possibility of teaming with colleagues, which can multiply the benefits of T-BAR. At this point, however, resist the temptation to select teammates. Let teams emerge from the process of developing plans. It may turn out that the best person for you to work with may be the one you least expect at the outset.

You may already have a plan in mind. Perhaps you identified one months ago. While this may be the exact plan of action you eventually carry out, keep yourself open to the possibility of change as you work with the rest of your group.

You have the ultimate professional responsibility to determine your actions as a teacher. Therefore, develop a plan of action from *your* values and experiences, a plan that you think will move your teaching closer to what you regard as good teaching. No one but you knows exactly what you believe good teaching to be.

Your plan should be designed to explore your ideas, not implement someone else's. T-BAR is not a technique for effecting an administrative policy, nor is it appropriate for testing another's curriculum or management program.

Your plan is not a traditional scientific experiment, either. It is neither necessary nor desirable to interrupt your instruction to conduct an experiment. After all, your plan of action is your attempt to improve your teaching, and you would not know the real effects of these changes unless you made them in the natural setting of your classroom. Only in rare instances would you change your behaviors in one class and not in others to determine the differential effect. Control groups, altered treatment of subjects, and other features of traditional educational research are not aspects of T-BAR. Why would you want to withhold your best teaching from some of your students?

A good plan promises to reveal the unknown. If your plan is likely to confirm something you already know, it is not really worth the effort of carrying it out. Formulate a plan about which, at this point, you can honestly say, "I know what I would like to happen, but right now, I really can't be sure that that is what will happen. Whatever the outcomes, though, the changes that I am going to make will definitely lead me to a clearer understanding of my students, my teaching, and myself."

T-BAR is not for pitting one ideology against another, so no T-BAR action plan can demonstrate that a behavioral approach is more valid than a cognitive one or that a democratic teacher is more effective than an authoritarian one. Proving a point is not the purpose of T-BAR. Opening new possibilities is. Understanding is. Insight is. Enlightenment is. It follows that you should keep the focus of your plan not on the dialectics of big issues in education, but on you. Select a plan of action that you can describe in this type of format:

> *What I believe good teaching is... What I am doing is... By changing my teaching behaviors in these ways... (or by exploring my situation in these ways...), I think that I can bring my teaching more in harmony with what I believe, and I will develop a deeper understanding of what I believe and why I teach the way that I do.*

While another person's answers are not likely to solve all your problems, do not assume that others' ideas cannot contribute to your teaching. You can benefit a great deal from the experience and creative thinking of others. Give serious consideration to the work of curriculum developers and classroom management experts. Analyze their thinking. Talk over their ideas with your group. Then use only what harmonizes with your goals and promises to meet the needs of your students.

Design your plan to be completed in five to ten class periods. This time is long enough to collect significant information about some effects of your actions and short enough to be flexible, so that you can change directions when your reflections result in new ideas.

Involve your students, too, in planning your actions. Tell them about your T-BAR group's area of concern. Explain your goals. Share your thoughts about how you might change your teaching. Describe the anticipated effects of your plan. Solicit their reactions to your proposals. Be open. The students are not your subjects. Ask yourself, "Why would it be in the best interests of my students for me to keep secrets from them?"

Checking Your Plan for Ethics and T-BAR Traits

The chances are practically nil that you would intentionally develop a unethical project. In planning changes in some principles of teaching, however, you will probably not be concentrating on their ethical dimensions. Now is a good time to think about such issues and review your plans from an ethical standpoint.

Strategy 7-1 presents ways that you can involve your T-BAR group in a discussion of the ethics of your action plan. Strategy 7-2 offers questions that you can ask yourself when reflecting on the ethics of your plan.

You can check your plan of action against the rating scale in Strategy 7-3 to determine how closely it matches the characteristics of a T-BAR plan. If your project does not closely exhibit T-BAR characteristics, you may want to rethink your plan and revise it or understand for yourself why your plan diverges from the T-BAR model.

All six strategies in this chapter are written as if you are formulating your plan alone. If you are teaming, meet for planning as a team, and then bring your work before the T-BAR group as a team.

Collecting Data

When your plan of action has been carried out, you will want to be able to answer two basic questions:

- How has the quality of education improved for my students?
- How has my understanding of my practice changed?

Complete and accurate answers to these questions require careful collection of information during the implementation of your plan. In fact, the value of T-BAR as a technique for improving teaching hinges on the thoughtful planning of data collection procedures, the collection of appropriate data, and the application of measures to ensure that results of the study are sound and credible.

Planning for Data Collection

Upon the completion of your study, you will want to have collected data that accurately represents the thoughts, feelings, and actions of the parties involved in your study. You will want that same kind of information, even if it is preliminary, while you are carrying out your research. This access to preliminary data will give you the ability to make informed changes of direction.

One logical approach toward the goal of accurate representation of effects involves following these steps:

1. Choose what you want to describe.
2. Decide what information you will need to do that accurately.
3. Select methods of getting and recording that information.

Strategy 7-4 provides a chart for helping you to work through these steps.

Methods of Collecting Data

A teacher carrying out typical classroom research is likely to limit data collection to impressionistic memories and end-of-unit test scores. The advantage of that approach over formal methods is that it does not take time away

Journals Several types of journals are described in some detail in Chapter 3. Journals used during your research can provide a record of changes during your project. Also, if you or your students have used journals in the past, your continuing to do so could reveal some interesting contrasts between past and present practice.

Portfolios Any systematic collection of materials about some aspect of your study can be considered a portfolio. The collection may include folders of student work, teaching plans, meeting minutes, or school announcements. One attractive feature of portfolios is that they often take very little time to compile.

Written snapshots These brief, but detailed, write-ups describe situations that jump out from the background of all that is going on. A well-chosen snapshot concentrates on an instance that seems significant but that has, at the time, an unknown or unclear meaning. Snapshots should be recorded as soon as possible after the incident. Feelings should be included. Later the snapshot can be read and interpreted.

Anecdotal records An anecdotal record is a written account of what has occurred over a period of time. It is more likely to be useful if it is written about a single person. Because the recorder needs to focus on the subject, an outside observer is usually required.

Audio and video tapes Tape recorders and video cameras can accurately capture classroom activities, often in an unobtrusive way. They record a lot of information with little effort, but transcribing this information so that it can be interpreted is very time-consuming. If these techniques are used for recording brief, potentially significant episodes, however, they can produce data that is both reliable and manageable.

Photographs One valuable use of photographs is as a focal point for discussions with students. The teacher might ask, for instance, "What were you doing (or thinking or feeling) here?" or "In which of these pictures were you more interested in schoolwork?"

Focused observations An aide or fellow teacher can record observations, which are most useful if the observer focuses on a single person or a particular aspect of activity. Sometimes observers use a checklist to record each time a certain behavior occurs. Focused observations may be directed toward taped, as well as live, sessions.

Interviews The most useful type of interview for T-BAR is one in which the interviewer has a half-dozen or so predetermined questions and asks other related questions to probe the respondent's answers. Interview-type questions asked during a whole-class discussion are likely to skew results, since the answers tend to reflect the views of only the most vocal students. Gathering data through class discussion, however, can save time and can sometimes reveal new areas for later exploration in individual interviews and questionnaires.

Questionnaires The frequent use of questionnaires as devices for gathering data in research projects is probably greater testimony to the ease by which they can be written, administered, and tabulated than it is to the value of the information that they provide. Before deciding to use a questionnaire, it is wise to think critically. Will a questionnaire really yield the type of information wanted? Would an alternative means of data collection work better?

Student tests The short-term nature of T-BAR and the typically low validity of teacher-made objective tests make test scores minimally useful as an evaluation device. The use of observations, interviews, and portfolios of student work usually provide richer evidence of student learning.

from teaching, which is an important consideration. Simply implementing your T-BAR action plan is going to require time and energy, and formal data collection only adds to that burden.

Trusting your memory alone, however, raises serious questions about the accuracy of your research findings, and you want to be reasonably sure of your results, since you are using them to draw inferences about your teaching performance. Furthermore, minimizing the importance of being precise and logical opens the entire T-BAR process to justifiable charges of being slipshod and unprofessional.

Thus, it is important to be realistic about what you can handle in your research. If T-BAR wears you down, you are less likely to ever use it again. A balance must be struck between ambition and feasibility. You must collect the information necessary to accurately describe what has happened—without interfering with the educational process and without consuming too much of the limited energy of all parties involved.

Figure 7.2 names and briefly describes some techniques for collecting information. They are possibilities for you to consider when you design the data collection component of your plan of action.

A Question of Validity You will need to build into your data collection approach some means of assuring its accuracy. Are your findings valid? Have you measured what you think you have measured, and are your results exact?

Your results are valid if they are:

- based on information that accurately represents the thoughts, feelings, and actions of those involved and

- derived logically from that information.

Figure 7.3 describes three techniques for promoting validity. Consider how, as members of a group, you can help each other collect data and ensure its validity.

Bear in mind, though, that techniques such as repeated observations and triangulation are not likely to yield identical data. Different observers will see different things, and they may describe what happens in very different ways.

These differences do not represent error. They do not mean that someone is wrong. They only mean that these differing viewpoints will make your description of what has occurred a more complex, complete, and valid reflec-

Repeated observations	Information is collected by several observers or by the same observer at several different times.
Triangulation	With this technique, the same phenomenon is viewed from two or more vantage points. Two ways of using triangulation are: • multiple investigators, who each use the same technique to gather information about the same event, and • multiple sources, which involves using two or more data collection techniques to gather information about a single event.
Participant checks	The persons about whom you have collected information are asked something like, "This is the data I have about your feelings (or thoughts or actions). Do my conclusions seem accurate to you?"

tion of the variety of ways that events are experienced.

Strategies 7-5 and 7-6 are included to help you think through your proposed data collection techniques from the standpoint of validity. Each strategy offers a structure that you can use to tell your group about your plans for dealing with validity concerns.

Implementing Your Action Plan

Now that you have been involved in repeated discussions and reflections on developing your plan of action, it is time to do what you have prepared to do. As you carry out your plan, always be prepared to change it if feedback suggests that you should. It is not necessary to pursue your plan to the end originally anticipated. Allow the problem to shift as it will.

Strategy 7-1
AN ETHICAL COMPARISON BY THE T-BAR GROUP

This strategy prompts you to consider the ethical implications of your T-BAR action plan.

If You Have a Statement of Ethics

If as a result of already completing some of the subsequent Chapter 7 strategies, you have formulated a written ethical statement:

• Compare that statement with your project plans and/or
• Give your group copies of your statement and action plan, and ask your colleagues if any aspects of your project seem to conflict with your ethical statement.

If You Lack a Statement of Ethics

If you do not have a written statement, ask your group to review your project plan for possible ethical violations.

Strategy 7-2
AN ETHICAL SELF-CHECK

This strategy presents a checklist for examining the ethical implications of a T-BAR action plan.

Yes, or No, But...

Check off the following items about your project if you are able to answer either "Yes" or "No, but it is ethical not to do so."

_____ 1. Does my project attempt to meet the needs of all of my students?
_____ 2. Will all of my students have an equal opportunity to learn?
_____ 3. Will all of my students have equal access to learning materials?
_____ 4. Will all of my students have an equal chance to succeed?
_____ 5. Will all of my students have the opportunity to make significant choices about their learning activities?
_____ 6. Will all of my students be listened to respectfully?
_____ 7. Do I expect all students' performances to be of high ethical and intellectual caliber?
_____ 8. Does the study maintain the strictest standards of confidentiality for everyone involved?

No, or Yes, But...

Check off the following items about your project if you are able to answer either "No" or "Yes, but it is ethical to do so."

_____ 1. Will I withhold information from my students about my intentions or the purpose of this project?
_____ 2. Will I withhold information from my fellow teachers about my intentions or the purpose of this project?
_____ 3. Will I withhold information from the school administration about my intentions or the purpose of this project?
_____ 4. Will I withhold information from parents about my intentions or the purpose of this project?
_____ 5. Is anything that I plan to do apt to harm my professional relationship with colleagues?
_____ 6. Is anything that I plan to do apt to bring any physical or emotional discomfort to any of my students?
_____ 7. Will I accept any student performance that is less than intellectually honest?

Strategy 7-3
RATE YOUR PROJECT

This strategy is useful for determining how consistent your action plan is with the T-BAR concept.

Rating

Using the scale below, assign the value of 0, 1, 2, or 3, according to the degree to which your plan of action matches each of the ten listed characteristics of T-BAR.

- 0 = no resemblance at all
- 1 = slight resemblance
- 2 = substantially similar
- 3 = practically identical

My plan is...

_____ 1. related to the T-BAR group's plan of action.
_____ 2. in harmony with what I consider good teaching.
_____ 3. realistically possible to carry out.
_____ 4. ethical.
_____ 5. likely to provide new insights into my teaching.
_____ 6. rooted in my values and experiences.
_____ 7. designed to benefit my students.
_____ 8. designed to interest my students.
_____ 9. designed to be carried out in a natural setting.
_____ 10. designed to show results in five to ten lessons.

Scoring

Total the numbers in the ten blanks. A 2 or a 3 on each characteristic and a total score of at least 25 points represents a good match between your project and a T-BAR plan of action.

Strategy 7-4
CHOOSING DATA COLLECTION TECHNIQUES

The chart in this strategy (Figure 7.4) is useful for systematically working toward accurate data collection.

Strategy 7-5
GROUP VALIDITY CHECK

With the chart in this strategy (Figure 7.5), you can check for validity of the data that you plan to collect.

In the left-hand column of Figure 7.5, briefly describe the kinds of data that you plan to collect. In the center columns, check each approach that you are going to use to ensure the validity of each type of data. In the right-hand column, briefly state what you think you can learn from each type of data.

What I expect to occur during the study:

	Expectation	What information will tell me it occurred?	How I can get that information	Q1	Q2
feelings					
thoughts					
actions					

What I expect to occur at the conclusion of the study:

	Expectation	What information will tell me it occurred?	How I can get that information	Q1	Q2
feelings					
thoughts					
actions					

Note. Q1 = Can I get this information without significantly interfering with the learning process?

Q2 = Can I get this information without unrealistic demands on my time and energy?

FIGURE 7.5: GROUP VALIDITY CHECK

Description of data I plan to collect	Types of validity checks				What I think this data can tell me
	1	2	3	4	

Note. 1 = Repeated observations; 2 = Triangulation by multiple investigators;
3 = Triangulation by multiple sources; 4 = Participant checks.

Strategy 7-6
GROUP DATA
COLLECTION
CRITIQUE

This strategy is used to solicit group feedback about your data collection plans.

The Plan Itself

Describe your plans for collecting data to your group. Ask the members to tell you if they believe that your action plan's techniques are:

- reasonably possible to implement and
- effective for gathering the designated information.

Alternatives to Consider

Then ask the group members if they think that there are:

- other techniques that you should consider and/or
- additional ways that the group could assist you in collecting data.

CHAPTER 8

REFLECTING ON YOUR RESEARCH

Thinking of teacher-based action research as a journey to a new place can be a useful metaphor. T-BAR, like a journey, has a destination. You have planned a route to the destination. Along the way, you may climb hills and see exciting new vistas. Or you may find yourself in strange territory with swamps, pitfalls, falling rocks, avalanches, violent storms, bad roads, and poor visibility.

With T-BAR, as with a journey, you expect some unexpected things to happen. Although you anticipate surprises, you can find yourself in some very uncomfortable predicaments. For this reason, this chapter presents some travel tips to smooth your way to the place where you want to go.

Reflection En Route

Carrying out your plan of action may require some of the busiest times that you have ever faced. Nevertheless, you should still meet with the T-BAR group on about the second and seventh day into this journey. An hour with the group can give you valuable encouragement and perspective.

Strategies 8-1 and 8-2 suggest a structure for these interim meetings. By responding to the statements in these strategies, you can pull back for a few minutes and reconsider some of what has happened.

Travelers' Innocence

Once your first plan of action has been completed, you will find yourself on higher ground. As you look back, you can see the path of your journey from a new perspective. You can also look ahead through new eyes. At this vantage point, it is time to bivouac and redraw your maps.

Your T-BAR group can help you now. One technique for deepening your reflection is to meet with the group as if you were a naive tourist. You are not, of course. From the experiences you have had with your T-BAR group, you have begun to gain new insights.

Withhold those insights. Tell you colleagues only about your expectations and experiences as if you have no clue as to what they mean. Let the group see your data, and allow them to interpret what they see and hear. Strategy

8-3 suggests one way to do this analysis (it can also be used to solicit students' opinions).

This device increases the likelihood of your gaining fresh ideas. Though it is true that the only useful meaning is the meaning you construct for yourself, withholding your insights while soliciting conclusions from the group will give you additional material from which to construct your new thoughts.

How Valid an Experience?

Chapter 7 stipulates two standards that your exploration must meet to be considered valid. The first, an accurate representation of what happened, can be met by including relevant data in a final report and conducting the group appraisal meetings during and after a project. The group critiques also serve as a validity check of the second criteria, the demand that any conclusions drawn be logically derived from the accurately represented data.

One ultrasafe way to meet the logic standard is to refrain from interpreting your data at all. You simply report the data without saying what you think it means. A strong argument can be made for abstaining from analysis. This viewpoint would assert that the researcher's job is to describe what happened, and it is the reader's responsibility to decide what the data means.

In teacher-based action research, such a position is not especially helpful. What it overlooks is that, in the T-BAR process, teachers will inevitably form conclusions. Keeping those thoughts private does not expose them to the scrutiny of others who can give valuable feedback.

For this reason, conclusions should be reported. The opinions of colleagues can be an important reality check. Let others assess how valid your insights are and how they might apply to other teaching situations.

While you do not want to draw firm conclusions that your data will not adequately support, permit yourself to speculate. Feel free to state your intuitions, so long as you identify them as such. For instance, you might preface suspected relationships with phrases like:

- I have little or no evidence for this, but I believe that...
- This notion goes beyond the study, but I think that...
- I have a hunch that if...
- It just might be that...

Such hypothetical leaps may help others see new possibilities. They also may suggest new directions for your next T-BAR journey.

The collective findings from your project are not likely to have the same universal validity sought in traditional research, but they are more than one person's opinion or even local solutions. Your record of your questions and struggles, in its openness, allows it to speak to readers with different beliefs and in different situations.

A New Itinerary

When you have rested and reflected on the meaning of your recent trip, it is time to meet with your group and scout new territory. If you were to stop the T-BAR process after carrying out only a single plan of action, you would not be taking advantage of the experience and momentum that you have just gained.

As a group, consider where you want to go next. Some guidelines for your discussion are suggested in Strategy 8-4.

Regrouping for Action

After the first round of action plans are implemented and the resulting data has been mined for implications, the T-BAR group may decide to restructure itself. For instance, you might form new groups around new areas of concern, or you might bring new members into the group.

With the membership of your group defined and an area of concern selected, you are poised to develop another plan of action. The information in Chapter 7 can help you to do that. Now that you are an experienced traveler, though, you may want to plan a project that will take longer than the five to ten days allotted to your first plan.

When the Road Ends

After several legs of this journey of research, you will reach a point where you want to set up camp, rest, and enjoy what you have learned in your travels. You will know when you reach that point. Maybe you will sense that your teaching has shifted to a higher plane. Maybe a whole new area of understanding will have fallen into place. Maybe the school calendar will call a halt. Something will tell you that you have come to the end of this line of research.

Compiling a Travelogue

At whatever point you stop your line of research, it is important that you record your experiences. The record of your research is vital to the T-BAR process for three reasons. In order of importance, they are:

- The process of developing a report facilitates your reflection.

Parts 1 to 4

The purpose of the first four parts of a typical T-BAR report is to provide an accurate representation of the thoughts, feelings, and actions of those involved in your research.

1. Our area of concern. As you begin writing, remember that, while the report's primary purpose is to aid your reflection, it can be much more than personal reminiscences. To make the report suitable for an audience beyond yourself, write as if you were informing other educators about your research.

2. What was happening in my teaching that was different from what I wanted to have happen. This section might be subdivided into three sections on:
- my beliefs and actions,
- the beliefs and actions of my students, and
- what I wanted to have happen.

3. What I changed or investigated. If you want to make lesson descriptions available, include them in an appendix, or tell the reader where to obtain them.

4. What happened. This section will be the most extensive part of the report. Organize your data around themes. Try to make it interesting. Rather than simply describing what happened, include excerpts of data from a variety of sources. A good rule of thumb is to include content that is about two-thirds data and one-third explanations, descriptions, and analysis.

Parts 5 and 6

The purpose of the last two parts is to relate some of your insights as a possible source of ideas for your colleagues. The purpose is not to prove a point or tell your readers what is certain to happen to them.

5. How the quality of education has improved for my students. Describe why you believe that your students now have a chance for a better education (even though the problems that you investigated may still exist).

6. How my understanding of teaching has changed. Think back to where you were before beginning your T-BAR activities. What differences are there between then and now? Why do you think that the changes you made work (or do not work)?

- The report serves as a basis for a T-BAR group critique of the project.
- The document can be a source of ideas for other educators.

Although you and your group are the primary beneficiaries of the process of report writing, construct the text as if your audience were educators who are not in your T-BAR group. The report should explain what you wanted to find out, what you found, and what conclusions you formed from the experience. Make the report interesting and meaningful to the reader. Logical organization and grounding general statements with illustrative, specific examples will help make the report readable. Figure 8.1 outlines a format for creating your report.

Although your report is likely to cover several plan-of-action cycles, write it as if it was a single research process instead of a series of disparate events. Be selective in what you describe, while still accurately representing the feelings, thoughts, and actions that took place.

That Others May Follow   Reporting your T-BAR work beyond your group has two major benefits. First, by publishing your report in some form, you invite the responses of fellow professionals. These responses comprise a wider test of the validity of your work and build your confidence in its value. Second, reporting on your research introduces the T-BAR process to more teachers and increases the chance that they will use it. In other words, your reflections and research can serve as a basis for other teachers' professional growth.

Unfortunately, at this time, few established channels publish accounts of T-BAR experiences, despite the keen interest that teachers involved in the process have in the insights of their counterparts elsewhere. The readers of national journals and the participants in national conventions are usually not classroom teachers engaged in T-BAR. As a result, these standard routes for the dissemination of educational research are not easily accessible to T-BAR teachers.

State-level professional conferences, however, are providing increasingly lively forums for action research reports. You are likely to get an invitation to present your findings if you submit a description of your work and request time for you, your team, or your entire T-BAR group. Another possible forum for you is the local chapter of a professional association.

If you choose not to seek an audience beyond your own T-BAR group, at least file a copy of your report in some place beyond your personal files. Likely places are the professional library in your building or with subject matter or grade-level supervisors at the district level. Cast your report upon the water. Some day, someone will read it and benefit from your experience.

Metaphor's End   Travelers on a journey usually reach a destination and stop. As a T-BAR traveler, on the other hand, you will not stop. You know that you are a better teacher than you were before T-BAR. You will also know, with confidence, why you are better. You can substantiate your improvement with evidence. Becoming your best, though, has no end. The more you understand, the more you want to find out.

Thus, at this point, the journey metaphor has reached the limits of its analogical aptness. It is time for you to finish the following sentence:

A more valuable metaphor to explain the way that I see myself as a teacher might be...

_____

_____

_____

Strategy 8-1
GROUP IN-
PROGRESS
MEETING 1
   This strategy provides a structure for a T-BAR group meeting to be conducted on or about the second day that you are executing your plan of action.

For You   *Prior to your* group meeting, complete the following sentences:

• Briefly stated, my plan of action is...

_____

_____

_____

• One specific change that I intended to make in my teaching behavior was...

_____

_____

_____

- Some evidence that I have made that change is...

_____

_____

_____

- When I made the change, one unexpected thing that happened was...

_____

_____

_____

- One way that I have already changed my action plan is...

_____

_____

_____

For the Group *Report your answers* to the preceding questions. Each member of the group should take no more than five minutes.

Decide exactly what kind of response you want from the group. As with the reports, responses should take no more than five minutes. Some possible requests for feedback are:

- Do you think that I changed my behavior in the way that I intended?
- How do you account for the unexpected result that I got?
- What particular data would you suggest that I look for?
- Might I have changed my plan in some other way than I did?
- What other changes in my plan might I consider making?
- What is one way that your experience has been the same as mine?
- Is there some way that you can encourage me?

Strategy 8-2
GROUP IN-
PROGRESS
MEETING 2
This strategy provides a structure for a T-BAR group meeting to be conducted on or about the seventh day that you are executing your plan of action.

For You   *Complete these sentences:*

- Briefly stated, my plan of action is…

_____

_____

_____

- One specific student feeling, thought, or action that I anticipated was…

_____

_____

_____

- Some evidence of what is occurring is…

_____

_____

_____

- Something that really pleases me about this study is…

_____

_____

_____

For the Group   *Report your answers* to the preceding questions. Each report to the group should take no more than five minutes. To encourage group members to lend their perspectives, set aside your own insights. Report only on the expectations that you had for your study, and present some of the data that you have collected.

Decide exactly what kind of response you want from the group. As with the reports, responses should take no more than five minutes. Some possible requests for feedback are:

- Do you see a way to get further verification that the specific thought, feeling, or action that I anticipated is actually occurring?
- In what ways is what is happening in my research similar to what is happening in yours?
- In the few days left in this phase of my study, what one thing would you advise me to look for?
- What is one thing that pleases you about my study?

Strategy 8-3
COMPILING
INSIGHTS

With this strategy, your group can help you gain fresh insights into the meaning of your study. *Note: To use this strategy effectively, you must first complete Strategy 7-4.*

For You

While your study is still underway, copy the information from the left-hand column of the table in Strategy 7-4 to the left-hand columns of the first two tables below. Then use data that you have just collected to complete the first table.

Feeling, thought, or action	*Did it happen?*	*How I know*
_____	_____	_____
_____	_____	_____
_____	_____	_____
_____	_____	_____
_____	_____	_____

As soon as your study has been completed and you have final data, complete this table:

Feeling, thought, or action	*Did it happen?*	*How I know*
_____	_____	_____
_____	_____	_____
_____	_____	_____
_____	_____	_____
_____	_____	_____

Also record the surprises of your study on this table:

A feeling, thought, or action
that I did not expect   *How I know that it happened*

_____   _____

_____   _____

_____   _____

_____   _____

_____   _____

For the Group *Present the information* in your tables to the group. Set aside your insights and encourage group members to give their perspectives. Report only on the expectations that you had for your study, and present some of the data that you collected. Instead of reporting on all of the expected results, focus on just one aspect of the study.

Ask the group questions such as:

- Do you think that what I believe occurred is what really happened?
- As you look at my data, do you think that any other significant feelings, thoughts, or actions occurred?
- As you consider everything that happened, what do you single out as the most important?
- In what ways do you believe that the quality of education for my students improved during this study?
- What did you learn from my study?

For You *Once you have* compiled your results and discussed them with your T-BAR group (and perhaps with students), reconsider the two basic T-BAR questions:

- How has the quality of education improved for my students?
- How has my understanding of my practice changed?

Write your best answers to these two questions, in your journal if you are keeping one. In any case, keep your answers for your own records.

Strategy 8-4
A New Direction

The purpose of this strategy is to help your T-BAR group to define a new direction for another round of action plans.

For You   *Complete these sentences:*

- Some of my new insights, pertinent to our group's area of concern, are...

_____

_____

_____

- Something within our area of concern (or outside our area of concern) that I would like to investigate is...

_____

_____

_____

- Possible changes in the area of concern are...

_____

_____

_____

For the Group   *In turn, report* your thoughts about the group's area of concern. Also discuss whether you want to keep your area of concern, reframe it, or identify an entirely new one. Finally, share your preliminary thoughts about possible new plans of action.

Strategy 8-5
Checking the Logic of Your Report

This strategy, which helps you doublecheck the logic of the conclusions that you drew from your study, will also help you to refine your report.

For You   *As you draft* your report, consider whether the conclusions that you have drawn are logical according to these criteria:

- You explicitly state the values related to your conclusions.
- You consider all relevant data.
- The data supports your conclusions.
- You do not claim that your conclusions are valid beyond your own practice.

Several days before your meeting, give the group members a draft copy of your report.

For the Group   *At your meeting,* ask the group members to ask questions about the logic of your report, in view of the previously stated criteria. Some examples of possible questions:

- On reporting values
    1. Are you aware of any beliefs that you have about students at risk for school failure that you haven't already told us about?
    2. You seem to have some rather strong views about the achievement of girls in school. Is that so?

- On considering all data
    1. Did you also see... happen?
    2. How did students with learning disabilities respond?
    3. It seems that you did not deal with... in your report. Why not?

- Supporting conclusions with data
    1. Couldn't this statement also be interpreted to mean... ?
    2. What evidence supports this statement?

- On limiting conclusions to your practice
    1. You state here that 5th grade students... Do you think that would be true of my 5th graders?
    2. In three places, you say, "Teachers should..." Aren't you going rather far with those claims?

ANNOTATED READINGS

Brubacher, John; Case, Charles; and Reagan, Timothy. 1994. *Becoming A Reflective Practitioner: How to Build a Culture of Enquiry in the Schools.* Thousand Oaks, Calif.: Corwin Press. Designed for use as a college textbook, this volume contains many short case studies of teacher reflection. It has a chapter on ethical decision making and another on reflection on community. This book could be useful to teachers who are interested in seeing examples of varying levels of teacher reflection.

Cohen, Rosetta Marantz. 1991. *A Lifetime of Teaching: Portraits of Five Veteran High School Teachers.* New York: Teachers College Press. This book portrays five teachers' lives (both in the classroom and out). The metaphorically rich quotations from these teachers could help other teachers recognize their own metaphors.

Cohn, Marilyn M., and Kottkamp, Robert B. 1993. *Teachers: The Missing Voice.* Albany, N. Y.: State University of New York Press. This report culminates an extensive study of teachers' views of what it means to teach today in the schools of Dade County (Miami), Florida. Chapter 9 presents a number of unanswered questions that could help T-BAR groups identify areas of concern.

Dollase, Richard. 1992. *Voices of Beginning Teachers: Visions and Realities.* New York: Teachers College Press. This study includes stories of four teachers, who are seen as player-coach, jazz musician, song leader, and storyteller. Seeing how the researcher isolated the metaphors from these teachers' words can be a valuable example for other teachers searching for their own metaphors.

Holly, Mary Louise. 1989. *Writing to Grow: Keeping a Personal-Professional Journal.* Portsmouth, N. H.: Heinemann. This volume on journal writing for teachers may inspire many teachers to begin recording their own professional growth. Three chapters are devoted to the journal-writing struggles of three primary-level teachers.

Kochendorfer, Leonard. 1994. "Biology Teachers As Researchers." *The American Biology Teacher* 56(3): 135-137. This article could be a useful tool for getting science teachers interested in joining a group to explore the use of teacher-based action research.

Livingston, Carol, ed. 1992. *Teachers as Leaders: Evolving Roles.* Washington: National Education Association. Stories of five teacher-led school restructuring efforts are featured in this work. The stories reveal an inspiring vision of what critical teachers can do.

Miller, Janet L. 1990. *Creating Spaces and Finding Voices: Teachers Collaborating for Empowerment.* Albany, N. Y.: State University of New York Press.

Miller met with a group of teachers as they examined their beliefs. This account of their experiences could be quite useful to a T-BAR group. Sections deal with doubts, felt boundaries, and looking to the future.

Newman. Judith M., ed. 1990. *Finding Our Own Way: Teachers Exploring Their Assumptions.* Portsmouth, N. H.: Heinemann.
Twenty-three teachers write about explorations into their teaching, chiefly the teaching of writing at the elementary and middle school levels. Some chapter topics are: questioning assumptions, making connections, reflecting, coping with conflict, changing, taking risks, and journeying.

Patterson, Leslie; Santa, Carol M.; Short, Kathy G.; and Smith, Karen, eds. 1993. *Teachers Are Researchers: Reflection and Action.* Newark, Del.: International Reading Association.
This collection, which includes 13 reports on elementary and secondary teachers' T-BAR projects, provides useful models for other teachers who are planning projects and reporting on them. Teacher reflection and research is also described.

Ross, E. Wayne; Cornett, Jeffrey W.; and McCutcheon, Gail, eds. 1992. *Teacher Personal Theorizing: Connecting Curriculum Practice, Theory, and Research.* Albany, N. Y.: State University of New York Press.
In the bulk of this book, education professors describe their work with classroom teacher reflection. Chapter 9 compiles the elements of six high school teachers' practical theories. Such information could help other teachers to clarify their theories.

Ruenzel, David. 1993. "Woman on a Mission." *Teacher Magazine* 4 (9): 26-31.
This profile of Lynn Sherkasky-Dave's struggle to gain her voice as a teacher may inspire others to continue with the critical process, especially when they feel stymied.

Schon, Donald A., ed. 1991. *The Reflective Turn: Case Studies in and on Educational Practice.* New York: Teachers College Press.
In Chapter 8, titled "Reframing," Russell and Munby describe a process that other teachers are likely to find themselves in. While the text is more abstract than concrete, it could provide insights about the value of the T-BAR experience.

Schubert, William H., and Ayers, William, eds. 1992. *Teacher Lore: Learning from Our Own Experience.* White Plains, N. Y.: Longman.
The professor-authors worked closely with teachers to help them formulate and write stories about their experiences. The respect that the editors show for the value of classroom teachers' knowledge might spur others on in dark times when they wonder if recording their lore is worth the effort.

Stevenson, Chris. 1986. *Teachers as Inquirers: Strategies for Learning with and About Early Adolescents.* Columbus, Ohio: National Middle School Association.
This brief, practical booklet serves as a guide to action research by classroom teachers. Although the process that Stevenson describes is not exactly like T-BAR, the brief accounts of 16 projects do provide a good framework for thinking about T-BAR projects.